MORE THAN

# 100
*favorite*
## DESSERT RECIPES

BY DR. DUANE LUND

MORE THAN

# 100

*favorite*

## DESSERT RECIPES

© Copyright 2014

By Lund S and R Publications, Staples, Minnesota 56479

First printing 2014

Printed USA, etc.

ISBN-13: 978-0-9740821-9-6
ISBN-10: 0-9740821-9-8

# Table *of* Contents

## CHAPTER 1
### *favorite desserts*

**PIE RECIPES**

**CAKE RECIPES**

## COOKIE RECIPES

## ICE CREAM DESSERT RECIPES

## CHAPTER 2
### *recipes from friends*

## CHAPTER 3
### *recipes from other countries*

### *German*

### *Scandinavian*

CHAPTER 1

# *favorite desserts*

# APPLE PIE

*Filling Ingredients*
**1/2 cup unsalted butter, melted**
**3 T all purpose flour**
**1/4 cup water**
**1/2 cup white sugar**
**1/2 cup brown sugar**
**6 medium size apples, peeled, cored, and sliced**

Spray bottom and sides of a 9 inch pie plate with cooking oil. Prepare crust in 350 degree oven (using your favorite recipe or one from this chapter). Combine all ingredients except apples, stir together and bring to a boil. Add all ingredients (with the apple slices on top) to the pan with the crust in it. Bake in a 350 degree oven 40 minutes until the apple slices are soft.

# BANANA CREAM PIE

3 T corn starch
3/4 cup sugar
2 cups milk
Dash of salt
2 T butter
3 egg yolks (beaten)
1 T vanilla extract
1  9 inch pie crust
5 bananas, sliced

In a sauce pan, combine the sugar, flour and salt. Gradually add milk while stirring until the mixture is bubbly. Cook (continue stirring) 2 more minutes.

Stir a little of the mixture into the egg yolks and add the rest of the egg yolk mixture to the rest of the hot mixture. Cook for 2 more minutes (remember to keep stirring). Remove the mixture from the heat and add the butter and vanilla. Stir until it has a smooth consistency. Slice the bananas into the baked pastry shell. Top with pudding mixture. Bake at 350 degrees for 15 minutes. Chill for an hour.

# BLUEBERRY PIE

*Crust Ingredients*
**2 cups all purpose flour**
**1 T salt**
**3/4 cup shortening**
**4 T cold water**

*Filling Ingredients*
**3/4 cup sugar**
**1/2 cup all purpose flour**
**1/2 T cinnamon**
**6 cups blueberries**
**1 T lemon juice**
**1 T butter, melted**

Mix flour and salt. Sprinkle in water. Stir with fork until all flour is moistened. Make a ball; divide in half; flatten and wrap in plastic; refrigerate 45 minutes. Heat oven to 400 degrees. Flatten with rolling pin and cover sides and bottom of pie plate.

Combine sugar, flour, cinnamon and blueberries. Sprinkle with lemon juice and butter. Cover with pastry topping and cut slits in it. Bake until crust is golden brown.

# CHERRY PIE

1 can cherry pie filling (21 ounces)
Package of cream cheese (8 oz.) softened
1 cup of milk (cold)
1 pkg. instant vanilla pudding
8 ounces cool whip, divided

Prepare a crust from your favorite recipe of from one of the recipes in this book. Spread 1/2 of the cherry filling over the bottom crust. Beat cream cheese until creamy. Add milk, slowly, until well blended. Stir in pudding mix. Stir in half of the cool whip. Spread over the cherries in the crust. Cover with the remaining cool whip and cherry filling. Refrigerate 4 hours. Do not cut until ready to serve.

# CHOCOLATE CREAM PIE

*Crust Ingredients*
**1 1/2 chocolate wager or cookie crumbs**
**5 T butter, melted**
**1/3 cup sugar**

*Filling Ingredients*
**Filing Ingredients**
**2/3 cup sugar**
**1/4 cup corn starch**
**Dash of salt**
**4 large egg yolks**
**3 cups milk**
**5 ounces bittersweet chocolate**
**3 ounces sweet chocolate, melted**
**2 T butter, softened**
**1 T vanilla**

TO PREPARE CRUST
Preheat oven to 350 degrees. Stir together crumbs, butter and sugar and press on sides and bottom of a 9 inch pie plate. Bake until crisp (about 15 minutes) and cool on rack.

TO PREPARE FILLING
Whisk together sugar, cornstarch, salt and yolks in a saucepan until combined well. Then add the milk, whisking as you add it. Bring to a boil over moderate heat, whisking, then reduce heat and let simmer, whisking for 1 minute (filling will be thick). Force filling through a fine mesh sieve into a bowl, then whisk in chocolate, butter and vanilla. Cover surface of filling with a buttered round of wax paper and cool completely. Spoon filling into crust and keep pie loosely covered at least 6 hours. Just before serving beat cream with sugar in a bowl until it just holds stiff peaks (use an electric mixer). Then spoon on top of pie.

# COCONUT CRÈME PIE

1  9 inch pie tin
2 1/4 cups whole milk
1 3/4 cup sugar, divided
3 eggs, separated
1/4 cup corn starch
1 t vanilla
1 3/4 cups toasted coconut
1 T butter

Heat oven to 400 degrees. Whisk the 2 cups of milk and 3/4 cup of sugar together in a saucepan. Over medium heat, bring liquid up to a simmer. Whisk the egg yolks together. Pour the hot milk into the egg yolks. Whisk the egg mixture and the hot milk mixture together. In a bowl, dissolve the corn starch in the remaining milk, making slurry. Whisk the slurry into the hot milk mixture. Bring the liquid up to a boil and reduce the heat to a simmer. As you cook the mixture, stir it until the filling is thick, about 5 minutes. Stir in the vanilla, coconut and butter. Pour the filling into the pie pan and cool completely. Using an electric mixer, whip the egg white to soft peaks. Add the remaining sugar and whip the egg whites into stiff peaks. Spread the egg whites over the top of the pie. Place the pie in the oven for a few minutes until the meringue is a golden brown.

# EGGNOG PIE

*Crust Ingredients*
**1/2 cup flour (all purpose)**
**1/2 cup finely chopped walnuts**
**4 T brown sugar**
**1 T cocoa**
**1 stick butter, melted (1/4 pound)**

*Filling Ingredients*
**1/2 cup sugar**
**2 T cornstarch**
**2 cups eggnog**
**2 1/2 gelatin (unflavored)**
**1/2 cup water (divided)**
**2 T cocoa**
**3/4 T rum extract**
**2 1/2 cups whipped cream**
**6 T ground nutmeg**

DIRECTIONS FOR CRUST

Preheat oven to 375 degrees. Mix together flour, walnuts, brown sugar and cocoa; then stir in the butter. Lightly coat your hands with cooking spray, and then press the mixture into a 9 inch pie plate. Bake for 10 minutes. Cool crust on wire rack.

DIRECTIONS FOR FILLING

Using a sauce pan for the filling, mix together the sugar and cornstarch. Mix in the eggnog, Cook over medium heat, stirring all the while, for 5 minutes, and then reduce heat to low and stir 3 more minutes. Remove from heat. In a micro-safe bowl, sprinkle gelatin over 1/4 cup water and microwave on high 20 seconds. Stir in Eggnog mixture. Divide mixture in half. In a bowl, whisk cocoa and remaining water. Stir into 1/2 eggnog mixture. Stir rum into remaining half. Refrigerate until set. Fold whipped cream into rum-flavored portion. Spread over the top. Sprinkle with nutmeg.

# FRENCH SILK PIE

**2/3 cup butter, softened**
**3 squares unsweetened chocolate#**
**1 cup sugar**
**1T vanilla extract**
**2 eggs**
**Melt, then cool**

Using  your favorite recipe, prepare a crust for a 9 inch pie tin.

Soften the butter in a mixing bowl. Gradually, stir in the sugar with an electric mixer. Stir in the cooked chocolate and vanilla extract. Stir the eggs in, one at a time.  Pour the chocolate filling into the pie shell.  Refrigerate before serving.

# HOLIDAY PIE (CRANBERRY AND APPLE)

3 t cornstarch
1 cup granulated sugar (divided)
1/4 cup brown sugar (firmly packed)
1 cup milk
1/2 cup thick cream
Yolks from 2 large eggs

Dash of salt
2 T butter
1/2 t vanilla extract
2 cups cranberries (fresh)
2 large apples, peeled, cored and cut into
small chunks

Use your favorite pie crust recipe or a recipe found in this book. Preheat oven to 375 degrees.

Line pastry with parchment paper, leaving an overhang. Top with weights (dry beans will work). Bake 30 minutes. Remove parchment (and weights). Bake another 10 minutes or until a light brown. Remove to a wire rack.

Prepare a custard by whisking together the cornstarch, 1/4 cup sugar and the next 5 listed ingredients in a large, heavy-duty sauce pan. Cook over low-medium heat, whisking all the while, for 6 or 7 minutes until thickened. Remove from the heat; whisk in butter and vanilla and cool. Combine cranberries, apples and remaining sugar in a sauce pan. Bring to a boil over medium heat. Cook over medium heat, stirring often for 15 minutes or until cranberries pop and apples are tender. Remove from the heat and cool. Spoon custard into pie shell and top with fruit mixture.

# HONEY PIE

1/4 pound (1 stick) butter, melted
3/4 cup sugar (granulated)
1 T cornmeal (white)
Dash kosher salt (or regular)
1 t vanilla extract
3/4 cup honey
3 eggs (large)
1/2 cup heavy cream (for whipping)
2 t white vinegar
2 T flake sea salt (If not available use regular salt)

Have ready a favorite 9 inch frozen pie crust of your choosing (or one found in this book). Preheat oven to 375 degrees.

Stir together in a bowl the melted butter, sugar, cornmeal, salt and vanilla. Stir in the honey and add the eggs one at a time, then the cream and vinegar.

Place the frozen pie shell on a baking sheet and strain the filling through a fine mesh sieve directly into the pie shell. Bake on the middle rack of the oven 45-50 minutes, rotating after about 30 minutes. The pie is ready when the edges are set and the center is no longer liquid but is a golden brown on top. Cool on a wire rack. Sprinkle with flake sea salt (or regular) and serve.

# KEY LIME PIE

*Filling Ingredients*
**1 stick (quarter Pound) butter, melted**
**1/2 cup lime juice**
**1 T lime rind, grated**
**1 can condensed milk**
**1 cup ice cream, softened**
**Yolks of 3 eggs**

*Crust Ingredients*
**1 T brown sugar**
**1 cup crushed graham crackers**
**2 T grated white chocolate**
**Dash of salt**
**3 T melted butter**
**1 T canola oil**

Spray bottom and sides of a 9 inch pie plate with cooking oil. Prepare crust in a 350 degree oven. Combine all crust ingredients and coat bottom and sides of pie plate. Bake 15 minutes, let cool. Whip together all filling ingredients except the ice cream. Pour into prepared pie crust and bake 15 minutes. Let cool, then cover with softened ice cream.

# LEMON MERINGUE PIE

*Filling Ingredients*
**Yolks of 4 eggs (save whites for meringue)**
**1 1/3 cups sugar**
**1 1/2 cups water**
**3 T butter (soft or melted)**
**1/3 cup corn starch**
**Dash of salt**
**1/2 cup lemon juice**
**1 T grated lemon zest**

*Meringue Ingredients*
**4 egg whites**
**1/2 t cream of tartar**
**2 T sugar**

Prepare crust in a 9 inch pie tin (use your favorite recipe or one found in this chapter) whisk egg yolks. Combine all other ingredients. Stir in egg yolks, and bring to a boil, stirring all the while (at least 1 minute). Pour into pie shell and cover with meringue. Make meringue by using a mixer. Beat egg whites until soft peaks form. Add sugar, gradually and continue for another minute.

# MINCEMEAT PIE

*Crust Ingredients*
**2 cups all purpose flour**
**1 T salt**
**1/2 cup shortening**
**4 T cold water**

*Filling Ingredients*
**2/3 cup coarsely chopped raisins**
**1/2 cup candied orange peel**
**1/4 cup brandy**
**Grated zest of one orange**
**1 T lemon juice**
**2 T brown sugar**
**1/2 heaping t of cinnamon**
**1/2 heaping t of nutmeg**
**1/2 t ground cloves**

TO PREPARE CRUST
Preheat oven to 400 degrees. Mix flour and
salt. Sprinkle in water. Stir with fork. Make a
ball; divide in half. Flatten and wrap in plastic.
Refrigerate 45 minutes. Flatten with rolling pin
and cover sides and bottom of pie plate.

PROCESS
Mix everything together and pack in a jar. Let stand, refrigerated, at least 3 days. If mixture
appears dry, add more brandy. Pour into prepared pie crust and bake 45 minutes. If you want to
cover pie with a crust, use same crust ingredients as above.

# PEACH PIE

*Crust Ingredients*
**1 3/4 crushed cracker crumbs (may use graham)**
**2 T sugar**
**3 T grated white chocolate**
**2 dashes salt**
**5 T melted butter**
**2 T canola oil**

TO PREPARE CRUST
Set oven at 350 degrees. Roll out dough with flowered rolling pin and place 2/3 of the dough in a 9 inch pie plate; leaving 1/2 inch hangover. Fold hangover under. Lightly prick bottom of pastry with a fork. Bake on middle rack 30 minutes and then let cool.

TO PREPARE FILLING
Use pre-heated oven. Stir together flour, sugar, and cinnamon and set aside. Wash, peel and slice peaches. Mix together peaches with dry ingredients. Turn into pastry-lined pie tin and dot with butter. Cover with top crust and cut wide slits in it. Seal the edges. Sprinkle top with sugar. Cove edges with foil to prevent burning. Remove foil for the last 15 minutes. Bake until brown (35 to 40 minutes)

# PECAN PIE

*Crust Ingredients*
**1 cup crushed cracker crumbs (may use graham)**
**1 T brown sugar (may use white)**
**2 T grated white chocolate**
**Dash of salt**
**3 T melted butter**
**1 T canola oil**

*Filling Ingredients*
**3/4 stick butter**
**1 1/4 cups of brown sugar**
**3/4 cup light corn syrup**
**2 T vanilla extract**
**1/2 cup grated orange zest**
**3 large eggs**
**2 cups pecan halves**

## TO PREPARE CRUST
Preheat oven to 350 degrees. Roll out dough with flowered rolling pin and plane in 9 inch pie plate; leaving 1/2 inch hangover. Fold overhang under. Lightly prick bottom of pastry all over with a fork. Bake on middle rack 30 minutes, and then cool.

## TO PREPARE FILLING
White crust is baking, melt butter, add brown sugar and whisk until smooth. Remove from heat and whisk in corn syrup, vanilla, and salt. Lightly beat eggs in a bowl, then whisk in corn syrup mixture. Put pecans in pie shell and pour syrup over them. Bake until filling is set (50-60 minutes)

# PUMPKIN PIE

*Crust Ingredients*
**1 1/3 cups all purpose flour**
**Dash of salt**
**1/3 cup vegetable oil**
**2 T cold water**

*Filling Ingredients*
**2 eggs**
**1/2 cup sugar**
**1 T cinnamon (ground)**
**Dash of salt**
**1/2 t ginger (ground)**
**Dash of ground cloves**
**1 15oz. can of pumpkin**

DIRECTIONS FOR TOPPING
Beat together 3/4 cup whipping cream and 3 T sugar using an electric mixer until stiff peaks form. Serve pie with whipped cream topping.

DIRECTIONS FOR CRUST
Preheat oven to 450 degrees. Mix flour, salt and oil. Sprinkle in cold water a little at a time. Shape pastry into a ball, then press on to bottom and up sides of a 9 inch pie plate

DIRECTIONS FOR FILLING
Beat eggs by hand. Beat in the sugar, cinnamon, salt, ginger, cloves, pumpkin and milk. Pour all the filling items down through the canned pumpkin into the pie plate. Bake 15 minutes, and then reduce heat to 350 degrees and bake for another 45 minutes. Cool for 2 hours on a rack.

# RASPBERRY PIE  (or other fruit)

**4 heaping cups of raspberries**
**1 cup sugar**
**1/3 cup flour**
**1 t grated lemon zest**
**1 T lemon juice**
**3 T butter**

Prepare crust using your favorite recipe or one found in this chapter and press into a 9 inch pie plate. Preheat oven to 350 degrees. Combine the sugar, flour and lemon zest in a bowl. Stir in the lemon juice and raspberries. Spoon the filling into the crust. Dot with little pieces of butter. Cover filling with crust dough. Crimp edges and bake until crust is golden (about 40 to 45 minutes)

# RHUBARB PIE

*Crust Ingredients*
**1 cup crushed cracker crumbs (may use graham)**
**1 T brown sugar (may use white)**
**2 T grated white chocolate**
**Dash of salt**
**3 T melted butter**
**1 T canola oil**

*Filling Ingredients*
**2 cups of rhubarb, cleaned and diced**
**2/3 cup sugar**
**2 T flour**
**2 egg yolks**
**2 T lemon juice**

Spray bottom and sides of a 9 inch pie plate with cooking oil. Prepare crust in a 350 degree oven. Combine all crust ingredients and coat bottom and sides of pie plate. Bake 15 minutes and let cool. Whip together all filling ingredients. Pour into prepared pie crust and bake 15 minutes. Let cool.

# SWEET POTATO-PUMPKIN PIE

*Ingredients for peanut pie crust*
**1 1/2 cups flour**
**Dash of salt**
**Peanuts (salted)**
**1/4 cup ice water**

*Ingredients for pie*
**1 3/4 pounds of sweet**
**potatoes**
**(rubbed clean)**
**1 can pumpkin puree**
**(15 oz)**
**3/4 cup sugar granulated**

**Dash of salt**
**1/2 t cinnamon (ground)**
**1/2 t nutmeg (ground)**
**4 eggs, beaten**
**1 cup buttermilk**
**2/3 cup whipping cream**

### DIRECTION FOR STREUSEL CRUNCH
Preheat oven to 250 degrees. Place a baking sheet lined with foil. Meanwhile, combine 1/2 cup crushed cheese crackers, 1/4 cup chopped peanuts, 2 T melted butter and 1 T brown sugar. Stir together. Spread on prepared baking sheet. Bake 25 minutes (stir half-way through) Cool.

### DIRECTION FOR PEANUT PIE CRUST
In a bowl, place flour, salt and peanuts. Use an electric mixer to combine. Add the cut-up butter. Pulse until pieces are pea size. With processor running, add 1/4 cup of ice water, one spoonful at a time until dough starts to come together. Knead mixture into a ball. Flatten dough on a floured surface. Roll into a 13 inch circle. Wrap the mixture around a rolling pin. Unroll into a 10 inch pie plate. Trim to 1/2 inch beyond edges of pie plate. Crimp.

### DIRECTIONS FOR PIE CONTENTS
Pre-heat oven to 375 degrees. Line a baking sheet with foil. Place sweet potatoes on foil and bake about 1 hour. Cool potatoes, then peel. Beat until smooth in a food processor. In a large bowl combine sweet potatoes, pumpkin puree, sugar, salt, cinnamon and nutmeg. Add eggs (beaten lightly), then stir in buttermilk and cream. Pour filling into prepared crust. Cover edge of piecrust with foil. Bake 375 degree oven for 50 minutes. Remove foil and bake 20 minutes cool completely. Serve with Streusel crunch.

# ANGEL FOOD CAKE

*Ingredients for a 10 inch cake*
**2 cups sugar (white)**
**1 1/3 cups cake flour**
**Dash of Salt**
**1 1/2 cup egg whites**
**1 T cream of tartar**
**1/2 T vanilla extract**
**1/2 t almond extract**

Beat egg whites until stiff peaks form. Add cream of tartar. Sift together salt, sugar and flour. Repeat this process five times. Combine (gently) the egg white with the dry ingredients. Pour into a 10 inch tube cake pan. Place in an unheated oven and then turn on the oben and set at 325 degrees. Cook for an hour or until the cake has turned a golden brown. Turn cake pan upside down and allow to thoroughly cool. Remove from pan and enjoy (various frostings may be added.)

# ANGEL FOOD CAKE WITH AN APPLE TOUCH

*Cake Ingredients*
2 cups sugar
3 eggs
1 cup oil
3 cups cake flour
1 T salt
1 T soda
2 T vanilla
3 cups chopped apples
1 cup walnuts, chopped

*Topping Ingredients*
1 cup brown sugar
¼ cup milk
½ cup margarine

Combine sugar, eggs and oil (beat together.) Beat in the dry ingredients and vanilla.

Stir in the chopped apples and nuts. Grease and dust a cake pan with flour. Bake for one hour in a pre-heated 350 degree oven. Let set a few minutes before turning out.

DIRECTIONS FOR TOPPING
Thoroughly mix ingredients then boil for 4 minutes. Let cool; it will thicken Drizzle over the baked cake.

# APPLE CRISPS

**2 large apples (hard variety, like Prairie Spy)**
**¾ cup brown sugar**
**5 Ts butter, melted**
**2 T lemon juice**
**¼ t vanilla extract**
**¼ t cinnamon (ground)**
**¼ t ground nutmeg**
**8 store-bought oatmeal or gingersnap cookies**

Instructions Go Here Instructions Go Here Instructions Go Here Instructions Go Here Instructions Preheat oven to 425 degrees.

Cut apples in half and core them. Cut the apples into thin slices. Place the apples, brown sugar, butter, lemon juice, vanilla, cinnamon and nutmeg in a bowl and toss until well coated. Divide mixture among four ramekins (round metal or otherwise oven-proof containers.) Arrange apple slices on top (fan shaped.)

Crumble the cookies and sprinkle over each of the four containers. Bake for 10 minutes or until apple slices are crisp but tender.

# BANANA-NUT CAKE

*Cake Ingredients*
2 cups flour (all purpose)
1T baking soda (level)
1T salt (coarse)
2 sticks (1/4 pound each) at room temperature
1 2/3 cups sugar
2 eggs
1 large ripe banana, mashed
1t vanilla extract
1 1/3 cups buttermilk
1cup nuts of your choosing (finely chopped)*
*Walnuts go well.

*Chocolate Glaze Ingredients*
1 1/2 cups powdered sugar
9 T cocoa (powdered)
3 T milk
2 t vanilla extract

Preheat oven to 350 degrees. Generously flour and butter pan (tube or Bundt or other.) In a bowl, combine flour, baking powder and salt. Combine butter and sugar and beat for 4 minutes with an electric mixer. Continue to beat as you add the eggs, one at a time. Beat in banana and vanilla. Add flour mixture and buttermilk alternately, beginning and ending with the flour mixture.(Mix until just combined). Stir in chopped nuts. Pour the batter into the prepared pan and smooth same. Bake 50 minutes. Let cool on wire rack for 10 minutes then remove and cool. To prepare glaze, whisk together sugar and cocoa. Stir in milk and vanilla (slowly). Whisk until smooth, and then spread over cake. Serves 12.

# CARAMEL, PUMPKIN AND PECAN CHEESECAKE

2/3 cup pecans, chopped
1 ½ gingersnaps, crushed fine
¼ cup melted butter
4  8 ounce packages of cream cheese*
1 cup sugar
1 can pumpkin (15 oz.)
1T pumpkin pie spice

1t vanilla extract
4 eggs
25 caramels*
1/4 cup milk

*Philadelphia brand works well
*Kraft brand works well

Preheat oven to 325 degrees.

Place the crushed gingersnaps in a bowl. Add butter and chopped pecans. Mix well. Press onto the bottom of a 9 x 13 inch pan.

Beat cream cheese and sugar in a bowl with an electric mixer until well blended. Add pumpkin, spice and vanilla. Mix. Add eggs, mixing well after each is added but at slow speed. Pour over crust.

Bake 45 minutes. Cool, then refrigerate 4 hrs. Microwave caramels and milk on high for 1 ½, minutes, stirring every 30 seconds. Spoon over each serving of cheesecake. Sprinkle with remaining nuts.

# CARROT CUPCAKES WITH ICING

1 1/2, cups whole wheat flour
1 t baking powder
1/2 t baking soda
1T cinnamon
½ t allspice
Dash of salt
3/4 cup canola oil

2 T butter
3/4 cup plain sugar
2 eggs
1 ½ t vanilla
1 ½ cups of grated carrots (fine)
1/4 cup chopped prunes
1 ½ cups confectioners' sugar
3 T skim milk

Preheat oven to 375 degrees. Line a 12 cup muffin pan with paper liners. Mix together the first six ingredients.

Using an electric mixer, beat together butter, oil and plain sugar in a bowl at medium speed. Add eggs, one at a time, continue beating after each addition. Stir in the vanilla. On slow speed add the flour mixture in 3 portions. Stir in the carrots and prunes. Fill each muffin cup and bake 25 minutes or until a wood toothpick comes out clean. Cool cupcakes.

Combine milk, butter and vanilla in a bowl. Stir in confectioners' sugar. Stir until icing is smooth, thick and glossy. Dip the top of each cupcake into the icing.

# CHEESECAKE, ANOTHER VARIETY

2  8 ounce packages of cream cheese
3 eggs, beaten (lightly)
1 10 oz package of vanilla cookies (crushed)
2 T sugar
6 T butter, melted
1 carton sour cream (8 oz.)

1 cup sugar (white)
3 T all purpose flour
2 t vanilla extract
½ T cinnamon (ground)
1 T sugar
½ t ground cinnamon

Allow cream cheese and eggs to stand at room temperature for 30 minutes. Preheat oven to 350 degrees. To make the crust, stir together crushed cookies and the T of sugar in a bowl. Then stir in the melted butter. Press the mixture onto the bottom and half-way up the sides of a 9 inch "spring-form" pan.

Beat together cream cheese, sour cream, 1 cup sugar, flour, vanilla extract and cinnamon with an electric mixer at medium speed in a bowl. Stir in the eggs.

In a small bowl, stir together the T of sugar and ½ t. cinnamon. Spread the cream cheese mixture into the pan (evenly) Sprinkle with the cinnamon mixture.

Bake at 350 degrees for 45 minutes. Cool on a wire rack for 15 minutes and then loosen from the sides of the pan with a knife. Cool 30 minutes more. Remove the sides of the pan and cool completely on the wire rack. Cover and chill 4 hours or more before serving.

Will serve 10-12.

# CHEESECAKE WITH DARK CHOCOLATE

1 1/2cup graham cracker crumbs
4 T sugar
1/2 cup melted butter
4 8oz packages of cream cheese*
1cup sugar
1t vanilla extract

4 eggs
1/2 pound whipping cream (whipped)
6 oz. chocolate chips
1cup raspberries or other favorite fruit

*Philadelphia brand works well

Preheat oven to 325 degrees.

Mix the graham cracker crumbs, sugar and butter and press onto bottom of 9 inch baking pan.

Beat together the cream cheese, 4 T sugar, and vanilla with an electric mixer. Add eggs, one at a time, mixing at slow speed. Pour over crust.

Bake 55 minutes. Run knife around rim of pan to loosen cake. Cool before removing rim. Refrigerate 4 hours.

Microwave whipping cream and chocolate chips in microwave bowl on high for 2 ½ minutes. Cool 15 minutes and pour over cheesecake. Sprinkle raspberries on top.

# CHEESECAKE SQUARES WITH FRUIT TOPPING

2 sticks butter (softened)
½ cup brown sugar (packed)
1/3 cup sugar
2 cups all purpose flour
1 1/3 cups finely chopped pecans

*Cheesecake Topping*
2  8 oz. packages of cream cheese
1/2 cup sugar
2 eggs
1 t vanilla extract
2T tequila (optional)
1T lime juice
1T lime zest
1T cornstarch
3 cups fruit (such as blueberries or
Raspberries or sliced strawberries)

Heat oven to 350 degrees.

Make crust by beating butter for a minute; then add both sugars and beat for another 3 minutes. Beat in the flour on slow speed 3 minutes. Stir in pecans.

Press the mixture evenly over the bottom of a 13 by 9 inch baking pan. Bake at 350 degrees for 10 minutes. Cool a little.

CHEESECAKE TOPPING
Beat cream cheese and sugar in a bowl for 3 minutes. Add eggs and vanilla and beat for 2 minutes. Beat in the tequila, lime juice and zest. Beat in the cornstarch.

Pour topping over crust. Bake at 350 degrees for 20 to 25 minutes. Cool slightly, then refrigerate I hr. Cut into 20 squares and refrigerate until serving. To serve, top squares with berries.

# CHERRY–BLUEBERRY SHORTCAKES

1 ½ cups fresh cherries, pitted
1 ½ fresh blueberries
1/2 cup sugar (granulated)
2 cups flour (all purpose)
1 ½ t baking powder
Dash of salt
1/3 cup butter

1 egg
2/3 cup whipping cream
1/3 cup honey
1/4 cup fresh cherries, pitted and chopped
1/4 cup fresh blueberries, chopped
Whipped cream (whip cream with ½ t vanilla)

Preheat oven to 400 degrees. Combine cherries, blueberries and sugar in a bowl. Set aside.

To make shortcakes, combine flour, baking soda, baking powder and salt in a large bowl. Using a blender, chip in the butter (small pieces). In another bowl, combine egg, cream, honey. 1/4 cup of the cherries and ¼ cup of the blueberries; add to the four mixture. Gently stir the mixture until the moistened "stuff' and dough come together.

On a floured surface, knead the dough until it holds together. Pat dough into 1/4 thickness. Using a cookie cutter (star or crescent or circle or some other shape of your choosing) cut into shapes you have chosen. Place shortcakes on an ungreased baking sheet. Bake for 12 minutes or until golden. Cool on baking sheet. Serve topped with berry mixture and whipped cream.

# CHOCOLATE CREAM CAKE

2 cups all purpose flour
1 cup brown sugar
1 cup white sugar
¾ cup cocoa
Dash of salt
Heaping T baking powder
Heaping T baking soda
3 T canola oil
1 cup mayonnaise

1 cup hot regular coffee
2 t vanilla extract
½ cup chocolate chips
Topping
10 T sugar
Dash cream of tartar
Dash of salt
½ cup chocolate syrup
6 eggs (whites only)

Preheat oven to 350 degrees. Combine first seven items. Add mayonnaise and oil; beat with an electric mixer at slow speed. Slowly add coffee and vanilla and continue to beat for another minute. Stir in chocolate chips. Pour into a 13x9 inch baking pan coated with cooking spray. Bake in pre-heated 350 degree oven for 30 minutes. Meanwhile, prepare the topping by combining all Ingredients with an electric mixer set at slow speed. Spread evenly over baked cake. (May substitute Whipped cream)

# CHOCOLATE NUT CAKES

Cooking spray (to prevent sticking)
8 T butter
1/2 pound chocolate chips
2 T finely chopped nuts of your choosing
3 T chocolate syrup
6 eggs (large and separated)
3/4 cup sugar
Whipped cream for topping when serving
1 cup chopped nuts of your choosing (hazel nuts work well)

Preheat oven to 325 degrees. Spray ramekins or other round, metal containers with cooking spray.

Combine butter (softened), chocolate chips, chopped nuts and chocolate syrup in a micro-wave safe bowl and microwave at 30 second intervals, stirring each time until melted. Whisk in egg yolks, 1 at a time. Put egg whites in a bowl and whisk by hand or with an electric beater until stiff peaks form. Beat in sugar. Mix half of egg whites into the chocolate mixture and then fold in the rest of the egg whites. Divide among the containers.

Bake until cakes pull away from the sides (about 40 minutes). Serve with whipped cream and chopped nuts on top.

# CORNMEAL PANCAKES AS A DESSERT

*Ingredients for Relish*
**1 ¼ pounds small tomatoes (seeded and chopped fine)**
**¼ cup basil, chopped fine**
**1 t olive oil**
**Dash of salt**
**½ t pepper (ground)**
**3 garlic cloves (minced)**

*Ingredients for cakes*
**1/3 cup all purpose flour**
**3 T cornmeal**
**Dash of salt (Kosher if available)**
**¼ t ground pepper**
**4 ½ T buttermilk**
**1 egg (large and separated)**
**Cooking Spray**

Combine first 6 ingredients for relish.

For pancakes: Combine the flour with the cornmeal, salt, and pepper (in a bowl). Combine the buttermilk and egg yolk. Add milk mixture to the flour mixture and whisk until moist.

Place the egg white in a bowl and beat with an electric mixer until peaks form. Fold ¼ of egg white into the buttermilk mixture. Fold in remaining egg white.

Heat a large skillet. (Medium heat).

Lightly coat pan with cooking spray. Spoon 1 T (just a little more) into the pan for each pancake. Spread lightly. Cook 1 minute or until tops are covered with bubbles. Turn and cook 1 minute. Repeat for about 16 pancakes. Top each with ½ t fresh or whipped cream and tomato relish.

# CUPCAKES WITH A HINT OF BACON

1 ¾ cups flour (all purpose)
¾ cup cocoa powder
2 ¼ t baking powder
Dash of salt
2 sticks butter (softened)
1 ¼ cup sugar (white)
3 eggs

1 T maple extract
¾ cup milk
10 slices thick cut bacon, chopped and fried crisp
1 cup chocolate chips
1 16 oz. box confectioners' sugar
2 more sticks of butter

Line two cupcake pans with 18 paper liners. Whisk together flour, cocoa powder, baking powder and salt. Beat together 2 sticks of softened butter and sugar; beat 3 eggs and 1 T maple extract. Beat in flour mixture, alternating with ¾ cup milk. Fold in 2/3 cups bacon (10 slices) chopped and fried crisp. Divide butter among liners and bake at 350 degrees 22 minutes.

Melt 1 cup chocolate chips and cool slightly. Beat together 1 box (16 oz) confectioners' sugar, 2 sticks of softened butter and ¼ cup of milk until smooth. Beat in the maple extract (1t) and chocolate.

Spread the frosting over the cupcakes. Garnish with the chopped, fried bacon

# DEVILS FOOD CAKE

1pkg. chocolate cake mix (Pillsbury works well)
1 can sweetened condensed milk
2 1ounce squares unsweetened chocolate, melted
½ cup water
1pkg. instant chocolate pudding mix (Pillsbury works well)
1 ½ cups whipped cream

Heat oven to 350 degrees. Prepare and bake cake mix according to directions on package. Beat chocolate and condensed milk until blended. Stir in water and pudding mix. Chill for 30 minutes. Stir in whipped cream. Chill for an hour. Lay one cake layer on a plate. Top with 1 ½ cups of the mixture. Place second cake layer on top. Cover sides and top with remaining mixture.

# FRUIT CAKE

**1 cup chopped or ground toasted pecans**
**2 cups flour (all purpose)**
**1 ½ cups sugar**
**1T baking powder**
**Dash of salt**
**½ cup milk**
**2/3 cup butter (softened)**
**2 eggs**
**2 apples, chopped (medium size)**
**1 cup dried apricots (chopped)**
**2 T ginger (fresh)**
**Optional: 3 T bourbon mixed with ¼ cup butter**

Preheat oven to 350 degrees. Grease and flour (lightly) 10 inch round or 9 inch square pan (spring form). Set aside. Combine ground pecans, sugar, flour, salt and baking powder (in a bowl). Add milk, butter, and eggs and beat with an electric mixer (low speed); then increase to medium speed for one minute. Fold in the dried fruit and ginger. Transfer to the prepared pan. Arrange the remaining chopped or ground pecans on top of the batter. Bake 40 minutes or until a wooden Toothpick (inserted) comes out clean. Cool in pan on wire rack 15 minutes. Remove sides of pan and cool completely. Remove bottom of the pan. If you choose to use butter-bourbon mixture, pour over fruitcake.

# FRUIT TOPPED ANGEL FOOD CAKE

1/2 cup brown sugar
3 T butter
1 pound fruit (pears, peaches or pineapple)
2 cups flour (all purpose)
1T ginger
2 T baking powder
Dash of salt
½ t cardamom (ground)
½ cup butter (softened)
1 cup sugar
3 eggs
1t vanilla extract
½ cup milk

Preheat oven to 350 degrees. Put butter in cake pan and put in oven and let melt. Spread melted butter around bottom of pan. Sprinkle with brown sugar. Cut fruit into narrow pieces about 1 ½ inches wide. Fan fruit slices over sugar with ends pointed towards center of the pan. Using a small bowl, stir together flour ginger, baking powder, salt and cardamom. Beat butter with an electric mixer until smooth. Add sugar and beat 2 minutes. Beat in eggs and vanilla. Beat in flour mixture. Spoon batter over fruit and spread with a spatula. Bake one hour at 350 degrees. Let cool a few minutes on rack. Invert cake onto plate.

# GINGERBREAD CAKE WITH FROSTING

*Cake Ingredients*
1 cup raisins
1 cup molasses
½ cup brown sugar
1/3 cup fresh boiled coffee
1/3 cup orange juice
1/3 cup canola oil
3 eggs

3 cups flour (whole wheat)
¼ cup powdered milk
1 T ginger (ground)
1 T orange peel, grated
1 t cream of tartar
1 t baking soda
½ t each ground mace,
cinnamon and nutmeg

*Frosting ingredients*
2 ½ cups confectioners sugar
4 T milk
2 T melted butter
¼ t vanilla extract

Preheat oven to 350 degrees. Grease and flour a 10 inch cake pan. Place the raisins in a bowl and cover with boiling water and let stand 5 minutes, then drain. In a bowl, whisk molasses, brown sugar, coffee, orange juice and canola oil. In another bowl, beat the eggs at high speed until thick. In a different bowl, whisk together the remaining cake ingredients. Add to the molasses mixture. Whisk in the eggs. Stir in the raisins. Transfer the batter to the prepared cake pan. Bake 55 to 60 minutes until an inserted toothpick comes out clean. Cool 10 minutes before removing to a wire rack to cool completely.

DIRECTIONS FOR FROSTING
Mix the frosting ingredients together until smooth. Pour evenly over cake.

# GREEN TOMATO AND FIG CUPCAKES

½ pound green tomatoes
  (quartered and cored)
2 cups cake flour (sifted)
1 t baking powder
½ t baking soda
½ t ground cinnamon
1 cup sugar

½ cup canola oil
2 eggs
2 t orange rind (grated)
1 cup figs, stemmed and
  chopped fine
2/3 cup chopped pecans
Cooking spray

*Frosting ingredients*
4 ounces cream cheese
  (with less fat)
1 ¼ cups powdered sugar
½ t vanilla extract
Dash of salt
½ cup sliced fresh figs

Preheat oven to 350 degrees. Blend tomato in a blender until smooth. Spoon flour into dry measuring cups; level with a knife. Combine flour, baking powder and baking soda, cinnamon and a dash of salt in a bowl. Place sugar, oil and eggs in a bowl and beat with an electric mixer at high speed. Stir in tomato puree and orange rind. Add flour mixture to egg mixture; beat at slow speed. Stir in figs and pecans.

Place 18 muffin cup liners in muffin cups; coat liners with cooking spray. Spoon batter into cups. Bake at 350 degrees for 18 minutes or until a toothpick comes out clean. Cool in pans 5 minutes. Remove from pans and cool completely on wire racks.

Beat cream cheese with an electric mixer at high speed. Add powdered sugar, vanilla and salt and beat until smooth. Spread frosting over top of cupcakes. Garnish with sliced figs.

# HERSHEY'S CHOCOLATE CHIP–BANANA CAKE

**4 eggs**
**1 cup Hershey's chocolate chips**
**1 cup water**
**1/2 cup vegetable oil**
**1 pkg. Hershey's banana cream pudding mix**
**1pkg Hershey's banana cake mix**

Heat oven to 350 degrees. Grease and flour 12 cup fluted tube pan.

Combine banana cake mix, pudding mix, eggs, water and oil in a bowl; beat on slow speed just until blended. Increase speed to medium; beat 2 minutes. Stir in chocolate chips. Pour batter into prepared pan.

Bake 45 - 50 minutes or until an inserted tooth pick comes out clean. Cool 10 minutes. Remove from pan to wire rack. Cool completely Drizzle with chocolate glaze.

CHOCOLATE GLAZE
Heat 1/3 cup sugar and ¼ cup of water in a small Sauce pan to a full boil. Stir until sugar dissolves. Remove from heat and add 1 cup chocolate chips. Stir with whisk until chips are melted and mixture is smooth. Cool to desired consistency, then use immediately over cake.

# HERSHEY'S CUPCAKES

**Dash of salt**
**2 T milk**
**1 1/4 cups berries (raspberries work well)**
**1/2 cup nuts of your choosing (crushed walnuts work well)**
**1 2/3 cups Hershey's white chips**

*Ingredients for Glaze*
**3/4 t baking powder**
**¼ t baking soda**
**1 egg**
**1 1/4 t vanilla extract**
**1 1/3 cups flour (all purpose)**
**1/3 cup light brown sugar**
**1/3 cup butter or margarine**
**1 cup sugar**

Heat oven to 350 degrees. Lightly grease or paper-line muffin cups. (1 3/4 inches in diameter)

Beat butter, granulated sugar, brown sugar and vanilla in a bowl until light and fluffy. Stir together flour, baking powder, baking soda and salt; gradually stir into butter mixture. Add milk and stir until blended. Stir in fruit, nuts and 2/3 cup white chips (reserve remaining chips for glaze. Fill muffin cups about 7/.8 full with batter.

Bake 18-20 minutes or until an inserted toothpick comes out clean. Cool 5 minutes; remove from pans to wire rack. Cool completely. Prepare glaze; drizzle over cakes.

To prepare white glaze, place remaining white chips and 2 T vegetable oil in a small bowl along with all listed ingredients for glaze.

In a micro-safe bowl; microwave on medium for 30 seconds; stir and microwave another 30 seconds. Drizzle over cupcakes.

# JELL-O 1-2-3 CHERRY POKE CAKE

**2 cups thawed cool whip**
**Whipped topping divided**
**1 loaf (16 oz) frozen pound cake thawed, room temperature**
**¾ cup boiling water**
**1 pkg (3oz) JELL-O Cherry Flavor Gelatin**
**¼ cup cold water**
**1 oz Baker's Semi-Sweet Chocolate**
**1 ½ cups cherry pie filling, divided**

Courtesy Jello.com Recipes

Pierce cake with a skewer at ½-inch intervals, poking skewer through cake to bottom of pan.

Add boiling water to gelatin mix in small bowl; stir 2 min. until completely dissolved. Stir in cold water; spoon over cake. Refrigerate 1 hour. Meanwhile make curls from semi-sweet chocolate.

Invert cake onto platter. Cut cake horizontally in half. Spread the bottom half of cake with 1/3 cup COOL WHIP; cover with 1 cup pie filling and top cake layer. Frost cake with remaining COOL WHIP. Garnish with remaining pie filling and chocolate curls.

12 servings

# LEMONADE ANGEL FOOD CAKE

3 level cups cake flour
Spray for coating pans
1 t baking powder
Dash of baking soda
Dash of salt
¾ cup buttermilk
1/2 cup milk
1 cup sugar

5 T butter, softened
3 T canola oil
2 egg yolks (large)
1 T grated lemon rind
3 egg whites
 Dash cream of tartar

*Ingredients for
lemonade syrup*
1/4 cup sugar
3 T lemon juice
2 T chopped lemon sections

Preheat oven to 350 degrees. Coat two 8 inch round metal baking pans with baking spray. Line bottoms of pans with wax paper and coat with baking spray.

Combine cake flour with baking powder, and salt in a bowl. Combine milk and buttermilk. Combine sugar, butter and oil in a bowl using an electric mixer until light and fluffy. Add egg yolks, one at a time. Beat in grated lemon rind. Add flour mixture and milk mixture alternatively.

Combine egg whites and cream of tartar using an electric mixer until peaks form. Fold egg white mixture into batter. Divide batter between two pans. Bake at 350 degrees about 25 minutes, until wooden pick inserted in middle comes out clean. Cool 15 minutes and invert on wire racks. Spread lemonade syrup between and over cakes.

# NO BAKE CAKE

**4 T butter**
**4 cups miniature marshmallows**
**6 cups Rice Krispies cereal**
**Frosting that comes in a can**
**Assorted miniature candies (such as chocolate chips)**

Melt butter in a sauce pan over low heat.

Add Rice Krispies. Stir until well coated. Using a butter-coated spatula, press mixture into a 13 x 9 inch pan, coated with cooking oil. Remove from pan.

Decorate with frosting and miniature candies.

# PLUM CAKE

**2 cups angel food cake flour**
**½ T nutmeg**
**½ T cinnamon**
**½ T cloves**
**3 eggs - well beaten**
**2 jars (small) plum baby food**
**1 cup vegetable oil**
**1 cup sugar (confectioners)**

Heat oven to 350 degrees. Sift the dry ingredients into a bowl. Add the plums, oil and eggs and blend. Pour into a greased cake pan and bake one hour in the pre-heated oven. Sprinkle the sugar on top.

# PUMPKIN CAKE ROLL

1cup flour (all purpose)
Heaping t spoon baking powder
2 t pumpkin pie spice (more for serving later)
Dash of salt
4 eggs
 ¾ cup sugar (white)
¾ cup canned pumpkin (puree)
1/2 cup confectioners' sugar

Preheat oven at 350 degrees. Coat a 15x10 inch with non-stick cooking spray, Line pan with wax paper and coat with spray. Wisk flour, baking powder, pumpkin pie spice and salt together in a bowl. With an electric mixer at medium speed, mix together eggs until it starts to thicken. Turn up to high speed and mix in granulated sugar a little at a time until thick and lemon-colored (about 6 minutes). At low speed, beat in pumpkin puree. Add flour mixture in two batches. Spread evenly in prepared pan. Bake at 375 degrees for 10 minutes or cake springs back when touched. Sprinkle ¼ cup Confectioners sugar on a towel. Loosen edges of baked cake and invert over towel. Remove pan and wax paper and sift remaining sugar over cake. From the short end, rollup cake with the towel. Let cool for an hour. Meanwhile, whisk pumpkin puree, 3 T sugar and egg yolk in a saucepan and cook for 5 minutes over medium heat. Transfer to a bowl and refrigerate 20 minutes. Once cake has cooled, unroll. Whip the heavy cream with 2 T sugar to stiff peaks. Fold in filling and spread over cake re-roll without towel. Whip remaining cream and sugar and spread over cake roll. Dust with pie spice.

# SPONGE CAKE

**4 eggs**
**¾ cup sugar**
**2/3 cup cake flour**
**¼ cup instant pudding mix**
**1 t cream of tartar**
**½ t baking soda**
**1/3 cup apricot or other jam**
**1 ¼ cups heavy cream, whipped**

Preheat oven to 350 degrees. Beat eggs and sugar with electric mixer until thick. Divide mixture between pans. Bake sponges 20 minutes. Turn top-side up onto parchment paper. Cool on wire rack. Make a sponge cake sandwich with jam and cream.

# STRAWBERRY ANGEL FOOD CAKE

1 19 oz. package Anglefood (white) cake mix
1 package strawberry Jello
Boiling water (1 cup)
½ cup cold water
2 cups whipped cream

Bake the cake in a 13x9 inch baking pan as directed on the package. Remove the baked cake from the oven and let cool for 30 minutes. Pierce the cake with a fork at half-inch intervals. Meanwhile, stir he boiling water into the dry Jello mix until completely dissolved. Add the cold water and pour over the cake. Refrigerate at least 2 hours. Cover with the whipped cream.

# STRAWBERRY SHORTCAKE (made with cornmeal)

**2 cups flour (all purpose)**
**1 cup cornmeal**
**1 ½ t baking soda**
**¾ t cream of tartar**
**Dash of salt**
**2 cups sour cream**
**1 egg**
**¼ cup sugar**

*Ingredients for topping**
**8 oz. mascarpone cheese**
**1 T sugar**
**3 T milk**
***May substitute whipped cream**

*Ingredients for filling*
**1 pound (16 oz.) fresh**
**strawberries, sliced**
**2 T sugar**

For the biscuits: Heat oven to 400 degrees. Lightly coat a large baking sheet with non-stick cooking spray.

In a bowl, whisk together flour, cornmeal, baking soda, cream of tartar and salt. In a smaller bowl, combine sour cream, egg and sugar. Make a "hole" in the dry ingredients and add sour cream mixture. Blend until the dry ingredients are moistened. Knead several times Drop ½ cup mounds of batter onto the prepared baking sheet. Bake at 400 degrees for 15 minutes or until an inserted wooden toothpick comes out clean.

Remove biscuits to a wire rack to cool. Directions for topping: Combine cheese, sugar and milk. Stir until smooth.* Directions for Filling: Combine sugar and strawberries. Top with cheese mixture.

# CAKE MIX COOKIES

**1/2 cup butter (1 stick)**
**2 eggs**
**1pkg. cake mix**
**2/3 cup quick-cooking oats**
**2/3 cup walnuts finely chopped**

Preheat oven to 375 degrees. Line baking sheets with parchment paper. In a bowl, mix butter and eggs until light and fluffy. Stir in cake mix, quick oats and chopped walnuts. Roll dough into balls the size of walnuts. Place cookies on baking sheet and flatten slightly. (The bottom of a glass that has been buttered and dipped in sugar works well) Bake 10 minutes in the preheated oven or until a golden brown. Allow cookies to cool a few minutes and then transfer to a wire rack to cool completely.

# CHOCOLATE CANDY BITS COOKIES

**2 sticks of butter (softened)**
**2/3 cup brown sugar**
**2/3 cup granulated (white) sugar**
**1 egg**
**1 1/2 t vanilla (extract)**
**2 cups of flour (all purpose)**
**1 1/4 t baking soda**
**Dash of salt**
**1 1/2 cups chocolate chip or M and M s**

Preheat oven to 350 degrees.

Using a large bowl, whisk butter and both kinds of sugar until thoroughly blended. Whisk in the egg and vanilla until thoroughly blended. Sift the flour, salt and baking soda together in a new bowl. Add these ingredients to the butter mixture and stir until well blended. Fold in the chocolate candies and chill at least one hour. Drop the dough by a well-rounded T spoon onto a lightly greased baking sheet about 2 inches apart. Bake about 10 minutes or longer if you want them crispy.

# CHOCOLATE CINNAMON COOKIES

**1 pound (16oz.) baking chocolate**
**3/4 cup flour**
**2 T roasted cinnamon (Saigon variety suggested)**
**1 t pepper (chili pepper suggested)**
**3/4 t baking powder**
**Dash of salt**
**2/3 stick of butter, softened**
**2/3 cup sugar (granulated)**
**1/3 cup brown sugar**
**2 eggs (lightly beaten)**
**2 t vanilla extract**

Melt half of the chocolate (suggestions on the package). Set aside. Chop (coarsely) the remaining chocolate. In a small bowl, mix flour, cinnamon, pepper, baking powder and salt. In a large bowl, beat butter and sugar with an electric mixer set on medium until light and fluffy. Add eggs and vanilla; mix well. Add melted chocolate; beat until well mixed. Gradually add flour mixture on low speed until well mixed. Stir in chopped chocolate. Drop dough by heaping tablespoons about 2 inches apart on baking sheets lined with parchment paper. Bake preheated 375 degree oven about 12 minutes or until cookies are set and slightly cracked on top. Transfer cookies on parchment paper to wire rack. Cool completely.

# COOKIES LACED WITH NUTS

**1 stick butter (softened)**
**½ cup brown sugar**
**2 T corn syrup (light)**
**3/4 cup flour (all purpose)**
**2/3 cup sliced nuts (like walnuts or pecans)**
**Dash of salt**

Preheat oven to 375 degrees. Combine butter, sugar and brown sugar in a small pan over medium heat. Stir until butter is melted. Remove from heat and stir in flour, nuts, and salt. Spoon heaping tablespoonfuls of batter onto cookie sheets lined with parchment paper. Line cookie sheets about 4 inches apart. Bake 375 degrees for 6 to 8 minutes until bubbly and a golden brown. Let sit on a baking sheet about 5 minutes, and then transfer to a wire rack to complete cooling. You may want to do this in 2 batches.

# CRANBERRY–CHOCOLATE–NUT COOKIES

¾ cup flour (all purpose)
Dash of salt
½ t baking soda
1 stick of butter (1/2 cup) melted
½ cup brown sugar
½ cup granulated (white) sugar
1 egg
1 t vanilla
1 ½ cups oatmeal
2/3 cup chocolate chips
½ cup sweetened cranberries (preferably dried)
2/3 cup chopped nuts (walnuts work well)

Preheat oven to 350 degrees. Whisk together four, salt and baking soda. Combine butter, both sugars, and beat slowly with an electric mixer. Add egg and vanilla and beat well. Add oatmeal and mix well. Add flour mixture (see second paragraph) Add oats, cranberries, chocolate chips and chopped nuts. Stir well. Drop dough by round spoonful, on to ungreased baking sheets. Bake 10 minutes or until golden brown. Let cool a couple of minutes, then remove to a wire rack to let cool completely.

# LEMON FLAVORED COOKIES

3 cups flour (all purpose)
½ t baking soda
Dash of salt
1 ½ cups sugar (granulated)
¾ cup of butter (softened)
1 egg
2 heaping tablespoons of finely shredded lemon peel
1/3 cup lemon juice
2 T finely cut rosemary
1 t lemon extract
½ cup powdered sugar

In a bowl, stir together flour, baking soda and salt. In a different bowl, beat together sugar and butter with an electric mixer until fluffy. Beat in egg, lemon peel, lemon juice, rosemary and lemon extract. Using the mixer beat in the flour mixture. (You may have to use a spoon to get it all in.) Divide dough into 4 portions. Shape each portion into a 6-inch log. Wrap each log with wax paper and twist the ends. Chill for at least 4 hours. Preheat the oven to 350 degrees. Line cookie sheets with parchment paper. Cut logs into quarter inch slices. Place slices about a quarter inch apart on the prepared cookie sheets. Bake for 9 or 10 minutes or until browned. Let cool a few minutes (2 or 3). Place powdered sugar in a bowl and turn 2 or 3 cookies at a time in the powdered sugar. Cool on wire racks.

# OATMEAL–PEANUT BUTTER COOKIES (SANDWICH)

½ cup brown sugar
¼ cup sugar (granulated)
2/3 cup peanut butter (chunky)
¼ cup shortening (vegetable)
Dash of salt
1 t baking soda
1 t vanilla extract
1 egg
1 cup rolled oats (not instant)
2/3 cup flour (all purpose)

*Peanut Butter Filling*
1 ½ cup, powdered
sugar (sifted)
2/3 cup of peanut butter
6 T milk

Preheat oven to 350 degrees. Line two baking sheets with parchment. Combine all ingredients except the flour. Using an electric mixer, beat until smooth. Add flour, beat at slow speed with electric mixer until well combined. Drop heaping tablespoons of dough on the baking sheets 2 inches apart. Using a table fork, flatten each cookie to about 3/8 Inch thick, making a crosspatch design. Bake 8 or 9 minutes, then transfer to a wire rack to cool. To make the peanut butter filling, combine all ingredients. Using the filling and two cookies for the top and bottom, make sandwiches.

# PEANUT BUTTER AND JELLY COOKIES

**1 cup of peanut butter**
**2/3 cup brown sugar**
**1/4 cup sugar**
**1egg (large)**
**1 t vanilla extract**
**Jar of strawberry jam**

Preheat oven to 350 degrees.

Beat peanut butter, sugar, egg and vanilla with an electric mixer and set at medium speed until well blended. Spoon heaping tablespoons of batter about 11/2, inches apart on a baking sheet lined with parchment paper. Flatten the dough (a fork works well). Make a half-inch indentation in the center of each cookie, using your thumb or a kitchen utensil but be careful to not push all the way through. Spoon a heaping teaspoon of strawberry jam into the center of each cookie. Bake 12 to 15 minutes or until cookies are a golden brown. Cool the cookies on the baking sheet for a couple of minutes. Transfer the cookies to a wire rack to cool completely before serving.

# TRIPLE CHOCOLATE PUMPKIN COOKIES

**2 sticks of butter**
**1 1/4 cups sugar**
**2 eggs**
**1/2 cup cocoa (powdered)**
**1 t pumpkin pie spice**
**1 cup pure pumpkin meat from the can**
**2 1/4 cups flour (all purpose)**
**Dash of salt**
**1 t baking powder**
**1/4 t baking soda**
**1 cup chocolate chips**
**1 cup chocolate chunks (semi-sweet)**

Using a bowl and an electric mixer, cream butter and sugar until well blended and fluffy. Add eggs and beat until well mixed. Stir in cocoa and pumpkin pie spice. Beat in the canned pumpkin. Stir in the flour, salt, baking powder and soda. Stir in the chocolate chips and chocolate chunks. Form dough into golf ball size chunks and place on lightly greased cookie sheets. Flatten into cookie shapes. Bake 16 to 18 minutes or until cookies look set. Transfer to a wire rack and cool completely.

# VANILLA COOKIES

1 ½ sticks (3/4 cup) melted butter
½ cup sugar (granulated)
Dash of salt (sea salt preferred)
3t vanilla extract
2 cups flour (all purpose)

*Powdered sugar icing:*
**In a small bowl, combine 1 ½ cups powdered sugar, ½ t vanilla and 4 t of milk.**

Line 2 cookie sheets with parchment paper. Beat butter, sugar and salt in a large mixing bowl, using an electric mixer set at medium-low speed for 1 minute or until smooth. Beat in the vanilla at slow speed. Turn off mixer and add the flour (all of it) Beat on slow speed until flour disappears into the dough. Using your hands, work dough into a ball. Divide into two halves. Using one dough peace at a time, roll between sheets of wax paper into ¼ inch thickness. Freeze between paper sheets for easier handling. In an oven preheated to 375 degrees remove one dough piece at a time. Let stand 5 minutes. Using cookie cutter of your desired shape, cut into desired shapes and place an inch apart on prepared cookie sheets. Bake one cookie sheet at a time 8 to 10 minutes until firm to the touch and golden brown on the sides. Decorate with powdered sugar icing, chocolate chips or other decorations as desired.

# BAKED POTATO ICE CREAM SUNDAE

**2 pints vanilla ice cream, softened**
**1 stick (1/2 cup) butter (softened)**
**1/4 cup sugar (confectioners')**
**10 drops yellow food coloring**
**1 cup of cocoa**
**2 cups whipped cream (for serving)**
**Chocolate sauce (for serving)**
**Dark green sprinkles (for serving; like chives)**

Have ready 4 sheets of plastic wrap. Place 3 generous scoops of ice cream on each sheet; gather ends lengthwise and mold into the shape of a baked potato. Set each on a sheet of aluminum foil and wrap to hold in place; transfer to freezer for one hour to firm. Repeat 3 more times.

In the bowl of an electric mixer fixed with a paddle attachment, cream butter and sugar until light and fluffy; mix in yellow food coloring. Using an offset spatula, spread butter 1/4 inch thick on a parchment lined baking sheet and freeze for 20 minutes. Cut into 1 inch butter pats and set aside.

Unwrap frozen "potatoes" and coat with cocoa powder. Draw a knife through the top of each potato to expose the inside. Top with whipped cream and green sprinkles (imitates chives) and butter pats. Serve with chocolate sauce.

# BROWN SUGAR CHOCOLATE CHIP ICE CREAM

**1/3 cup Egg Beater or other pasteurized egg product**
**1 1/2 cups heavy cream**
**1/2 cup milk**
**1/2 cup brown sugar**
**2 t vanilla extract**
**1/2 cup chocolate chips**
**1/2 cup chopped pecans**

Combine all ingredients, blending well. Pour into ice cream freezer and follow manufacturer's directions for freezing ice cream. Pack into a container and store in freezer. Makes about 4 cups.

# COFFEE ICE CREAM PIE

*Ingredients for crust*
**30 Oreos or other chocolate wafers (crushed)**
**1/2 cup butter, softened**
**1/4 cup coconut (shredded)**
**4 T nuts, chopped (cashews work well)**

*Ingredients for filling*
**1 quart coffee ice cream, softened**
**Ingredients for Topping**
**1 cup hot fudge topping, warmed**
**Whole cashews or favorite nuts**

In a medium bowl, mix crushed Oreos, butter, coconut and chopped nuts. Press mixture in bottom and side of a 9 inch glass pie plate. Refrigerate 15 minutes. Carefully spoon softened ice cream into chilled crust. Cover and freeze 2 hours. Top individual servings with fudge topping; garnish with nuts. Cover and freeze any remaining pie.

# COOKIE DOUGH ICE CREAM SAMMIES

**4 Kellog's Pop Tarts Frosted Chocolate Chip Cookie Dough Pastries**
**1 heaping cup ice cream**
**2/3 cup whipped cream**
**4 T chocolate chips**

Cut Kellog's pop tarts chocolate chip cookie dough into halves. Top unfrosted sides of toaster pastry pieces into 1/4 cup of the ice cream and spread carefully. Spoon dollop of whipped cream on each. Sprinkle with chocolate chips. Top with an additional toaster piece, unfrosted side down. Lightly press together, making four "sandwiches."

# COOKIES AND ICE CREAM CHEESECAKE

1 pkg. chocolate chip cookies (15.2 ounces)
2 T butter melted
2 pkgs Philadelphia Cream Cheese (8oz ea.) Softened
1/2 cup sugar
2 t vanilla extract
6 cups vanilla ice cream

Crush 20 cookies (fine crumbs); mix with butter. Press into bottom of 9 inch spring form pan. Chop 16 of the remaining cookies. Beat cream cheese, vanilla, and sugar in a large bowl with a mixer until blended. Add ice cream; mix well; stir in chopped cookies; pour over crust. Freeze 4 hours or until firm. Remove from freezer 10 minutes before serving. Let stand at room temperature to soften slightly. Top with remaining cookies.

# MUDDY BUDDIE'S BROWNIE ICE CREAM
## (a Betty Crocker Recipe)

6 cups vanilla ice cream
10 chocolate chip cookies, crumbled
1/3 cup chocolate flavored syrup
1 10.5 ounce bag Chex Mix Muddy Brownies Supreme Snack Mix

In a large bowl, mix ice cream, crumbled cookies, and two cups of the snack mix. Freeze at least 1 hour until firm. For sundaes, scoop a generous 1/2 cup of ice cream mixture into each serving bowl. Drizzle each with 1 T chocolate syrup; top with remaining snack mix.

# NO BAKE BANANA SPLIT CAKE DESSERT

*Ingredients for the crust*
**2 cups graham crackers, crushed**
**1/2 cup butter, melted**
**Ingredients for the cream cheese layer**
**12 oz cream cheese**
**1/4 cup sugar (granulated)**
**8 oz whipped cream**

*Ingredients for the fruit and topping*
**4 bananas sliced**
**1  20 oz. can of crushed pineapple**
**16 strawberries (sliced)**
**6 cups ice cream**
**1/2 cup chopped walnuts**

Grease a 9x13in. baking dish; set aside. In a bowl, combine graham crackers and melted butter. Dump into prepared pan. Press into an even layer; refrigerate. In a bowl, mix together cream cheese and sugar. Fold in the whipped cream. Spread on top of the graham cracker crust. Arrange banana slices on top of the cream cheese filling. Top with a layer of crushed pineapple and then a layer of sliced strawberries. Cover with a layer of ice cream. Sprinkle with chopped walnuts.

# OREO ICE CREAM DESSERT

**30 Oreo cookies, crushed**
**1/2 cup melted butter**
**Carton of Cool Whip**
**1/2 gallon ice cream (any flavor)**
**1 can chocolate fudge topping**

Mix butter and crushed Oreos. Spread in 9x13 inch pan. Slice ice cream and spread over cookies. Pour fudge topping over ice cream. Spread Cool Whip over top. Sprinkle with crushed Oreo crumbs. Freeze 20 minutes between each layer.

# PEACH CRISP A LA MODE

3 large fresh peaches, peeled and sliced
1 cup plus 2 T pancake baking mix, divided
1 cup brown sugar, divided
3/4 T ground cinnamon, divided
1/2 t vanilla extract
Dash of salt
1 cup sliced almonds
1/2 stick butter (1/4 pound) sliced into 1/2 inch cubes
3 cups vanilla ice cream

Preheat oven to 375 degrees. Combine peaches, 2 T baking powder mix, 1/3 cup brown sugar, 1/4 T cinnamon, vanilla extract, and dash of ground salt in a bowl. Divide evenly between 6 ramekins (8-10 ounces). Place on a baking sheet and set aside. Combine remaining 1 cup baking mix, 2/3 cup brown sugar, 1/2 T cinnamon and dash of salt with almonds in a medium bowl. Add butter (chopped) and cut with a pastry blender or 2 knives. Press together with fingers until clumps form. Sprinkle evenly over peach mixture. Bake 30 minutes or until bubbling in center and topping is golden. Serve topped with ice cream.

# TURTLE BROWNIE ICE CREAM DESSERT

### Brownies
**1 box Bettey Crocker
   fudge brownie mix
Water, vegetable oil and
   eggs as called for on box
1/2 cup pecans, chopped**

### Filling
**2 quarts (8 cups) de leche ice cream, softened
1/2 cup Hershey's hot fudge topping, warm
2/3 cup pecans, chopped
1 cup thawed whipped topping**

Heat oven to 350 degrees. Spray bottom of 15x10x1 inch pan with cooking spray. In a large bowl, stir brownie mix, water, oil and eggs until blended. Stir in 1/2 cup pecans; spread in pan.

Bake 16 minutes. Cool completely on a wire rack for about 45 minutes. Spoon ice cream evenly over brownies. Smooth with the back of a spoon. Freeze uncovered about 3 hours. To serve, drizzle hot fudge topping over dessert with fork. Using quick strokes. Sprinkle with 2/3 cup of pecan pieces. Let stand at room temperature about 5 minutes before cutting. Serve topped with whipped topping.

# VERY BERRY SUNDAE

3/4 pint strawberry ice cream
3/4 pint raspberry and/or strawberry sorbet
1/2 cup raspberry sauce
1/2 cup marshmallow sauce
1/2 pint raspberries

Line two small baking pans with parchment paper. Using a miniature ice cream scoop, scoop strawberry ice cream, placing scoops on prepared pan; transfer to freezer. Repeat process with sorbet. Let scoops freeze 30 minutes. Arrange scoops of ice cream and sorbet among 4 dishes; top with raspberry sauce, marshmallow sauce and raspberries. Serve.

# *recipes from friends*

# PETER'S FAVORITE RHUBARB DESSERT

*Courtesy Eva Joy (Lund)*

1pkg. graham crackers crushed
1/4 cup melted butter, mix together
Put 3/4 of the mixture In a 9X13 inch pan.

Cook- 4 cups of rhubarb
1 cup of sugar
1/2 cup water
3 Tbsp. cornstarch
Cool this mixture and add 1/2 package raspberry jello powder.

Spread rhubarb mixture over graham cracker crust.

Whip 1 cup whipping cream and mix in 2 cups miniature marshmallows.
Spread over rhubarb layer.

Mix 1-3 oz. package of instant vanilla pudding with 1 1/2 cups milk.
Spread over marshmallow layer.

Top with remaining graham cracker crumbs.

# DANNY'S FAVORITE DELUXE CHEESECAKE

*Courtesy Eva Joy (Lund)*

Crust: 1cup graham crackers (crushed) (6)

1/4 c. butter melted
1/4 c. sugar
(Pat Into the bottom of a 9" spring form pan)

Base: 2 lb. cream cheese
1 egg slightly beaten
1cup sugar
1/2. tsp. Almond extract
1tsp. vanilla

Place in a cold oven. Turn to 350 degrees. Bake 1/2 to 3/4 hour.

Topping: 1 pint sour cream
3/4 c. sugar

1tsp. lemon juice

After baking, pour on topping gently. Put back in oven for 10 min. May be shaky.
Refrigerate until cool.

# JACK'S FAVORITE PISTACHIO DESSERT

*Courtesy Eva Joy (Lund)*

**1cup flour**
**1stick butter**
**2 Tbsp. sugar**
**Mix together and spread in 9X13 inch pan. Bake 15 minutes at 350. Cool.**

Mix 8 oz. cream cheese, 2/3 c. powdered sugar. Add 1/2, carton of Cool Whip (9 Oz). Place this on top of crust. Mix 2 pkgs. Of pistachio instant pudding mix and 2 1/2 cups milk; spread over the above layer. Spread the other 1/2, of Cool Whip over this layer. Sprinkle the top with grated semi sweet chocolate.

# EVA JOY'S FAVORITE COOL LEMON SQUARES

*Courtesy Eva Joy (Lund)*

**1 1/4 c. graham cracker crumbs or crushed vanilla wafers**
**1/4 cup sugar**
**1/4 cup butter (melted)**
**3 egg yolks**
**1(14 oz.) can sweetened condensed milk**
**1/2 cup Real lemon juice from concentrate**
**Yellow food coloring (opt.)**
**8 oz. cool whip**

Preheat oven to 325. Combine crumbs, sugar and butter. Press firmly in 9X9 pan or pie tin. In small bowl beat egg yolks, condensed milk, lemon juice and coloring. Pour into crust and bake 30 min. Cool completely. Top with whipped topping. Refrigerate or freeze. These are good topped with strawberries or raspberries. Fresh or frozen. Make a large pan by simply doubling the ingredients.

# RED VELVET CAKE

*Courtesy Max Rutger*

*CAKE*
*Cream until fluffy:*
**1 1/2 c sugar**
**1/2 c butter**

*Fold in and beat until smooth:*
**3 T cocoa**
**2 eggs**
**1/4 c red food coloring**
**1 tsp salt**
**1 tsp vanilla**
**1 tsp soda**
**1 tsp vinegar**
**1 c buttermilk**
**2 c flour**

Bake at 350 for 30 minutes (round cake) or 35-40 minutes (9x13'pan). Let layers cool, then split each with thread.

*FROSTING*
*Cream until fluffy:*
**1 1/2 c sugar**
**1 1/8 c butter**

*Cook, beating with wire whip until thick:*
**1 1/2 c milk**
**4 1/2 T flour**
**Let cool, then fold into butter-sugar mixture slowly.**

*Add:*
**1 tsp vanilla**
**1/2 tsp almond**

Beat until smooth. Frost cake and enjoy!

# PUMPKIN PIE DESSERT

*Courtesy Sharon Silker*

*1st Layer:*
**1 Box yellow cake mix (save 1 cup for topping)**
**1/2 cup butter**
**1 egg**
**Mix together & place in 9x13" pan**

*2nd Layer:*
**28oz pumpkin**
**1 cup sugar**
**4 eggs**
**1 tsp vanilla**
**1 1/2 tsp cinnamon**
**1/2 tsp ginger**
**1/4 tsp cloves**
**Mix together & add to pan.**

*Topping:*
**1 c cake mix (saved from above)**
**1/4 cup sugar**
**1/2 tsp cinnamon**

**Bake at 350 degrees for 45 minutes.**

# RHUBARB CREAM PIE

*Courtesy Julia Davies*

**2 T butter**
**1 1/4 cup sugar**
**2 T flour (rounded)**
**2 eggs (beaten)**
**4 to 6 cups rhubarb (cut up)**

Cream butter and sugar. Add beaten eggs then mix in the flour. Add rhubarb. Fill unbaked pie shell.

Bake at 400-425F for 10 minutes, then another 35-45 minutes at 350F.

This filling will form its own crust. Serves 6-8.

# ORANGE CRANBERRY BARS

*Courtesy Betsy Hayenga, Waite Park*

1/4 cup all-purpose flour
1 1/2 t sugar
2 T cold butter
2 T chopped nuts of your choosing

In a bowl, combine flour and sugar; cut in butter until mixture resembles coarse crumbs. Stir in pecans. Press into an 8x4x2 inch loaf pan coated with nonstick cooking spray. Bake at 350 degrees for 15 minutes.

*Topping:*
2 T beaten egg
1 1/2 t milk
3/4 t grated orange peel
1/4 t vanilla extract
1/3 cup sugar
1 1/2 t all-purpose flour
1/4 cup fresh or frozen cranberries
2 T flaked coconut
2 T chopped pecans

Meanwhile, in a bowl, combine the egg, milk, orange peel, and vanilla. Combine sugar and flour, gradually add to egg mixture and mix well. Fold in the cranberries, coconut and pecans. Spread over crust. Bake 15-20 minutes or until golden brown.

# CARMEL CORN OLD DUTCH STYLE

*Courtesy Julia Hayenga*

**1pkg. Old Dutch Popcorn 9 oz.**
**1 cup butter**
**1 1/4 cups brown sugar**
**2/3 cup light corn syrup**
**1T baking soda**
**1 cup nuts (whole cashews)**

Preheat oven to 250 degrees.

Combine butter, brown sugar and corn syrup in a 2 qut. Sauce pan. Cook on medium heat until mixture has melted, then add baking soda.

Pour pufcorn and nuts into a large roasting pan. Pour caramel mixture over pufcorn and mix thoroughly. Place in oven for 45 minutes and stir every 10-12 minutes.

Remove from oven and place on wax paper and break apart. Let cool.

# LOU WILSON'S YUM YUM APPLESAUCE CAKE

*Courtesy Jack Wilson*

**Whip 1/2 cup of shortening into a cream.**
**Add 1 cup of sugar, mix with cream.**
**Add one cup unsweetened apple sauce and stir into apple sauce.**
**Add 1T baking soda.**
**Add 1 1/2 cups flour.**
**Add 1T cloves.**
**Add 1T cinnamon**
**Add 1 T nutmeg**
**Add raisins and 1 cup nuts (optional) (May be chopped)**

Bake in tube pan, 40 minutes at 350 degrees.

# CHOCOLATE CAKE

*Courtesy Jim and Mary Vogel*

*This recipe is dedicated to the memory of Bernice Vogel.*

**3 c. flour**
**2 c. sugar**
**2 tsp. baking soda**
**I tsp. salt**
**1/3 c. cocoa**
**2/3 c. oil**
**2 T. vinegar**
**2 c. strong hot coffee**

Mix dry ingredients together. Add remaining ingredients and mix well. Pour batter into 9x13-inch pan, which has been sprayed with Pam or buttered. Bake at 350 degrees for 30 to 35 minutes.

This cake has no eggs, but a very moist cake.

*Praline Frosting:*
**1 c. brown sugar, firmly packed**
**4 T. flour**
**1/2 cup butter**
**1/2 cup cream (1/2 & 1/2)**
**4 egg yolks**
**1 T. vanilla**
**1 1/2 cups coconut**
**1/2 cup pecans**

Mix flour and cream together till smooth. Melt butter, add brown sugar, egg yolks, cream and flour, and cook till thick. Add vanilla and let cool. Frost cake.

# CARMEL BROWNIES

*Courtesy Patty Tindall (Allrecipes.com)*

**1 pkg German Chocolate cake mix**
**1 1/2 sticks butter, softened**
**1 sm can sweetened-condensed milk**
**1 pkg caramels**
**1 1/2 c chocolate chips**

Mix cake mix, butter, and half can condensed milk
Take half batter and pour into 9x13 pan
Bake at 350 for 6 minutes
Melt caramels and mix in rest of milk
Pour over cooled cake
Sprinkle chocolate chips over top
Spread rest of batter over all and bake 15 minutes more

# SEVEN LAYER BARS

*Courtesy Patty Tindall (Allrecipes.com)*

1/2 cup unsalted butter
1  1/2 cups graham cracker crumbs
1 cup semisweet chocolate chips
 1 cup butterscotch chips
1 cup  chopped walnuts
1 (14 ounce) can sweetened condensed milk
1 1/3 cups shredded coconut


1. Preheat oven to 350 degrees F (180 degrees C).

2. Place butter in 13 x 9 inch pan and melt in oven. Swirl to coat bottom and sides with butter.

3. Spread crumbs evenly over bottom of pan. Layer chocolate chips, butterscotch chips, and nuts over crumbs. Pour condensed milk over nuts. Sprinkle coconut over condensed milk.

4.  Bake until edges are golden brown, about 25 minutes. Let cool.

# COCONUT CREAM DESSERT

*Anonymous*

*Crust:*
**1c flour**
**1c butter, softened**
**1c chopped walnuts or pecans**

**Mix softened butter with flour and nuts, put in 9x13 pan and bake at 350 degrees for 20 minutes or until light brown. Cool.**

*1st Layer:*
**1c powdered sugar**
**8oz cream cheese**
**1/2 of an 8oz container of cool-whip**
**Whip together and spread on cooled crust.**

*2nd Layer:*
**2 small boxes coconut cream instant pudding**
**2c milk**
**Blend together until thick. Spread on top of 1st layer.**

*Top:*
**Top with remaining cool-whip. Sprinkle toasted coconut over cool-whip.**
**Refrigerate.**

# LEMON CAKE WITH LEMON FILLING AND LEMON BUTTER FROSTING

*Courtesy Anela via Eric Peterson (Allrecipes.com)*

2 c. all-purpose flour
2 tsp. baking powder
1 tsp. salt
1/2 c. butter
1 1/4 c. white sugar
3 eggs
1 tsp. vanilla extract
1 c. milk

1 tbsp. grated
 lemon zest
1/2 c. fresh
 lemon juice

1 tbsp. cornstarch
6 tbsp. butter
3/4 c. white sugar
4 egg yolks, beaten

4 c. confectioners' sugar
1/2 c. butter,
 softened
2 tbsp. fresh
 lemon juice
1 tsp. grated
 lemon zest
2 tbsp. milk

1. Preheat oven to 350 degrees F (175 degrees C). Grease and flour two 8 inch round pans. Mix together the flour, baking powder and salt. Set aside.

2. In a large bowl, cream together the butter and sugar until light and fluffy, about 5 minutes. Beat in the eggs one at a time, then stir in the vanilla. Beat in the flour mixture alternately with the milk, mixing just until incorporated.

3. Pour batter into prepared pans. Bake in the preheated oven for 30 minutes, or until a toothpick inserted into the center of the cake comes out clean. Allow to cool in pans on wire racks for 10 minutes. Then invert onto wire racks to cool completely.

4.  To make filling: In medium saucepan, mix together 1 tablespoon lemon zest, 1/2 cup lemon juice and 1 tablespoon cornstarch until smooth. Mix in 6 tablespoons butter and 3/4 cup sugar, and bring mixture to boil over medium heat. Boil for one minute, stirring constantly. In small bowl, with a wire whisk, beat egg yolks until smooth. Whisk in a small amount of the hot lemon mixture. Pour the egg mixture into the sauce pan, beating the hot lemon mixture rapidly. Reduce heat to low; cook, stirring constantly, 5 minutes, or until thick (not to boil).

5. Pour mixture into medium bowl. Press plastic wrap onto surface to keep skin from forming as it cools. Cool to room temperature. Refrigerate 3 hours.

6. To make frosting: In large bowl, beat confectioners' sugar, 1/2 cup butter, 2 tablespoons lemon juice and 1teaspoon lemon zest until smooth. Beat in milk, and increase speed and continue to beat until light and fluffy.

7. To assemble: With long serrated knife, split each cake layer in half horizontally, making 4 layers. Place 1 layer, cut side up, on a serving plate. Spread with half of the lemon filling. Top with another layer, and spread with 1/2 cup frosting. Add third layer, and spread with remaining half of the lemon filling. Press on final cake layer, and frost top and sides of cake with remaining frosting. Refrigerate cake until serving time.

# CHOCOLATE KAHLUA CAKE

*Courtesy Cindy Adams*

**1 chocolate cake mix**
**1 chocolate instant pudding (small box)**
**4 eggs**
**1/3 c  Kahlua**
**3/4c oil (or applesauce)**
**2 c sour cream**
**6oz chocolate chips**

Blend all ingredients and pour into greased cake or bundt pan.

Bake at 350 for 50-60 minutes.

Bake at 325 if using a dark, non-stick pan.

# CHOCOLATE CHIP COOKIES

*Anonymous*

1 cup granulated sugar
1 cup brown sugar
1 cup ( 2 sticks) butter or margarine, softened
2 eggs
1 1/2 teaspoons vanilla
1 teaspoon baking soda
1 teaspoon salt
3 cups all-purpose flour
12 ounces semi-sweet chocolate chips

Place sugars, butter, eggs, and vanilla in mixer bowl. Attach bowl and flat beater to mixer. Turn to Speed 2 and mix about 30 seconds. Stop and scrape bowl. Turn to Speed 4 and beat about 30 seconds. Stop and scrape bowl.

Turn to Stir Speed. Gradually add baking soda, salt, and flour to sugar mixture and mix about 2 minutes. Turn to Speed 2 and mix about 30 seconds. Stop and scrape bowl. Add chocolate chips. Turn to Stir Speed and mix about 15 seconds.

Drop rounded teaspoonfuls onto greased baking sheets, about 2 inches apart. Bake at 375 degrees for 10 to 12 minutes. Remove from baking sheets immediately and cool on wire racks. Convection 350 degrees for 10 minutes.

# RHUBARB UPSIDE-DOWN CAKE

*Courtesy Martha Stewart*

*For the Topping:*
**4 tablespoons unsalted butter, melted**
**1/2 cup all-purpose flour**
**1/4 cup sugar**
**Coarse salt**

*For the Cake:*
**1 1/2 sticks unsalted butter, room temperature,**
 **plus more for buttering pan**

**1 pound rhubarb, trimmed and cut on a very**
 **sharp diagonal about 1/2 inch thick**

**1 3/4 cups sugar**
**1 1/2 cups all-purpose flour**
**1 1/2 teaspoons baking powder**
**Coarse salt**
**1/2 teaspoon finely grated orange**
 **zest plus 1 tablespoon**
**fresh orange juice**
**2 large eggs**
**1 cup sour cream**

1. Preheat oven to 350 degrees. Make the topping: Stir together butter, flour, sugar, and 1/4 teaspoon salt until moist and crumbly.

2. Make the cake: Butter a 9-inch round cake pan (2 inches deep). Dot with 4 tablespoons butter (cut into pieces). Toss rhubarb with 3/4 cup sugar; let stand for 2 minutes. Toss again, and spread in pan.

3. Whisk together flour, baking powder, and 1 1/2 teaspoons salt. Beat remaining stick butter and cup sugar with a mixer on medium speed until pale and fluffy. Beat in zest and juice. Beat in eggs, 1 at a time, until incorporated, scraping down sides of bowl. Beat in flour mixture in 3 additions, alternating with sour cream, until smooth. Spread evenly over rhubarb. Crumble topping evenly over batter.

4. Bake until a toothpick inserted into the center comes out clean and top springs back when touched, about 1 hour. Let cool for 10 minutes. Run a knife around edge of cake, and invert onto a wire rack. Let cool completely.

# PUMPKIN CHEESECAKE

*Courtesy Paula Dean*

*Crust:*
**1 3/4 cups graham cracker crumbs**
**3 tablespoons light brown sugar**
**1/2 teaspoon ground cinnamon**
**1 stick melted salted butter**

*Filling:*
**3 (8-ounce) packages cream cheese,**
 **at room temperature**
**1 (15-ounce) can pureed pumpkin**
**3 eggs plus 1 egg yolk**
**1/4 cup sour cream**
**1 1/2 cups sugar**
**1/2 teaspoon ground cinnamon**
**1/8 teaspoon fresh ground nutmeg**
**1/8 teaspoon ground cloves**
**2 tablespoon all-purpose flour**
**1 teaspoon vanilla extract**

Preheat oven to 350 degrees F.

FOR CRUST: In medium bowl, combine crumbs, sugar and cinnamon. Add

Melted butter. Press down flat into a 9-inch spring form pan. Set aside.

FOR FILLING: Beat cream cheese until smooth. Add pumpkin puree, eggs, egg yolk, sour cream, sugar and the spices.

Add flour and vanilla. Beat together until well combined.

Pour into crust. Spread out evenly and place oven for 1 hour. Remove from the oven and let sit for 15 minutes. Cover with plastic wrap and refrigerate for 4 hours.

# CARAMEL APPLE PIE

*Courtesy Midwest Living*

**If apples are sliced thicker than suggested, they won't be done in the baking time allotted.**

Use favorite recipe for single-crust pie
1 1/3 cups all-purpose flour
2/3 cup sugar
1/3 cup cold butter, cut into small pieces

1 cup sugar
1 teaspoon ground cinnamon
2 1/4 pounds apples, peeled, cored and cut into 1/4-inch slices (about 6 cups)
1/2 to 3/4 cup dulce de leche ice cream topping, or caramel ice cream topping, slightly warmed
1/2 cup coarsely chopped walnuts or pecans, toasted
Whipped cream or vanilla ice cream (optional)

1. Prepare and roll out pastry. Line a 9-inch pie plate with pastry. Trim overhanging edge to an even 1 inch all the way around. Tuck the crust under and flute the edge. Do not prick pastry. Line pastry with a double thickness of foil; add pie weights, if you like. Bake in a 400 degree oven for 15 minutes to partially bake pastry shell. Remove foil and pie weight. Reduce oven temperature to 375 degrees

2. For crumb topping: In a medium bowl, stir together flour and 2/3 cup sugar. Using a pastry blender, cut in cold better until mixture resembles coarse crumbs. Set aside.

3. In a large bowl, stir together 1 cup sugar and cinnamon. Add apple slices. Gently toss until coated. Transfer apple mixture to partially baked pastry shell. Press fruit gently with your hands to provide a relatively flat, mounded surface on which to add the crumb topping. Sprinkle crumb topping over apple mixture. To prevent overbrowning, loosely cover pie with foil.

4. Place pie plate on middle shelf in oven; place foil-lined baking sheet on lower rack beneath pie. Bake in 375 degree oven 30 minutes. Remove foil. Bake 40 to 50 minutes more or until fruit is tender, filling is bubbly and crumb topping is golden brown. Cool on a wire rack at least 2 hours before serving.

5. To serve, drizzle with warm ice cream topping and sprinkle with nuts. Serve with whipped cream or vanilla ice cream, if you like. Makes 8 servings.

Note: To replace the dulce de leche ice cream topping, in a small saucepan, heat and stir 3/4 cup vanilla caramels and 1 tablespoon half-and-half or light cream over low heat until melted and smooth.

# RED VELVET CAKE

*Anonymous*

*For the Cake:*

**Cream until fluffy (5 minutes)**

| | |
|---|---|
| 1 1/2 c | sugar |
| 1/2c | butter |

**Fold in and beat until smooth:**

| | |
|---|---|
| 3T | cocoa |
| 2 | eggs |
| 1/4 c | red food coloring |
| 1tsp | salt |
| 1tsp | vanilla |
| 1tsp | soda |
| 1tsp | vinegar |
| 1c | buttermilk |
| 2c | flour |

Bake at 350 for 30 minutes (round cake) or 35-40 minutes (9x13 pan). Let layers cool; store cake in refrigerator for 2 days (to moisten). Split each with thread.

*For the Frosting:*

**Cream until fluffy:**

1 1/2c sugar

1 1/8 c butter

**Cook, beating with wire whip until thick:**

1 1/2c milk

4 1/2T flour

**Let cool; fold into butter-sugar mixture slowly.**

**Add:**

1tsp vanilla

1/2tsp almond

Beat until smooth. Poke holes in cake; frost and enjoy!

# STRAWBERRY PRETZEL DESSERT

*Courtesy Donna Miller*

1 1/2 cups crushed pretzels
1/2 cup sugar
1/2 cup melted margarine
8 oz. cream cheese
1 cup sugar
8 oz. cool whip
2 3oz. packages strawberry jello/ 2cups hot water
2  10oz.pkgs. frozen strawberries

Combine first 3 ingredients and pat into pan. Bake at 375 degrees for 7 minutes.

Cream in cheese and sugar and fold in 8 oz cool whip. Spread on cooled crust and refrigerate.

Mix strawberries into strawberry jello. Spread on cool whip layer. Serve with a dollop of whipped cream.

# BLACK FOREST DESSERT

*Courtesy Donna Miller*

**1 German chocolate cake mix**

**2 - 8oz. pkgs. Philadelphia Cream Cheese**
**2 - 3 1/2 oz.pakgs.vanilla instant pudding mix 2 cans. (3 cups) cherry pie mix**
**2  8oz. cartons Cool Whip**
**1 lg. Hershey Bar, grated**

Mix cake mix as directed on the box. Pour into two 9 x 13 inch pans. Bake  20 minutes at 350 degrees. Cool.

Beat pudding mix with 3 cups of milk until creamy. Set aside.

Cream the cream cheese and blend pudding mix into cream cheese a little at a time. Pour over cakes. Pour pic filling over pudding mix and spread and then spread cool whip over the top. Top with grated Hershey bar.

Refrigerate. (may freeze)

# FORGOTTEN LEMON DESSERT

*Courtesy Judy Droubie*

Beat six egg whites, 1/4 tsp salt until foamy.
Add I/2 tsp cream of tartar until stiff.
Add 1tsp vanilla.
Add 1 1/2cups sugar one Tbs. at a time as you beat.

Spread in an un-greased 9x12 pan.
Put in oven preheated to 450.
Turn off oven and let cool over night.
DO NOT OPEN OVEN UNTIL MORNING.

Make lemon mixture to spread over top in the morning.
Lemon mixture:
Mix 6 egg yolks, 2/3 cup of sugar, 4 Tbs. lemon juice and cook until thick.

Cool and spread over top and add layer of Cool Whip (8 oz).

CHAPTER 3

# *recipes from other countries*

# CREAM CAKE

*Courtesy Name Here*

**1 ¼ cup Granulated Sugar**
**½ cup lard or shortening**
**¾ teaspoon salt**
**1 teaspoon vanilla**

Place sugar, lard, salt, and vanilla in large mixing bowl. Cream well.

**2 Eggs**

Add eggs one at a time, beating well after each addition.

**¼ cup Cocoa Powder**

Add cocoa and blend well.

**1 ¾ All purpose flour, sifted**
**1 teaspoon Baking Powder**
**1/4 teaspoon Baking Soda**
**1 cup Evaporated Milk, undiluted**

Sift together flour, baking powder and baking soda. Add flour to creamed mixture, alternately with evaporated milk, beginning and ending with the flour. Mix well between each addition. Pour batter into two 8 inch round greased and floured cake pans. Bake 350 degrees for 25-30 minutes. Remove from oven, cool. Cut layer into 2 layers to yield 4 layers total.

**1 ½ cups Heavy Whipping Cream**
**1 teaspoon Vanilla**
**4 Tablespoons Powdered Sugar**

Combine these three ingredients and whip until stiff. Use between layers and on top of 4th layer. Refrigerate cake 2-3 hours.

# CHOKECHERRY JELLY

**10 Cups or 3 ½ pounds Chokecherries, raw, cleaned with stems and leaves removed**
**2 Apples, raw, cut in eighths**
Place cleaned chokecherries and apple pieces in large stainless steel pot. Add just enough water to barely cover berries and apple pieces. Bring to boil and simmer with lid on pot for 30 minutes. Arrange 2 layers of cheesecloth in a colander that is set in a large stainless steel pot. Pour cooked fruit and juice into colander containing cheesecloth. Collect juice into the pot. Discard cooked fruit solids. Measure 3 ½ cups juice. Use this to make jelly.

**6 Jelly jars**
**6 Lids**
**6 Rings**
Before you start cooking juice with SURE JELL, you must start sterilizing jars, lids, rings by doing the following: Place jars, rings and lids in large pot and set pot on burner on stove. Fill pot and jars with water. Bring to a boil and keep on medium boil until ready to fill with jells. (See below)

**3 ½ cups cooked, strained chokecherry juice**
**1 package SURE JELL**
**4 ½ cups Granulated cane sugar**
While jars, lids and rings are being sterilized (see above) do the following: Place juice in large stainless steel pot. Add SURE JELL and stir until dissolved. Bring to boil and boil for one minute while stirring constantly.

# BREAD PUDDING

**6 slices stale bread (but not moldy!)**
**2/3 cup raisins**
**6 medium crisp apples, cored, peeled and sliced (thin)**
**1 stick butter, sliced thin (1/4 pound)**
**3 T sugar (divided)**
**2 T cinnamon**
**4 T flour**
**3 cups milk**
**3 eggs**

Arrange 3 slices of bread on bottom of a baking dish that has been lubricated with butter. Stir together with apple slices, raisins, 1 ½ T sugar and cinnamon. Distribute over bread slices and top with remaining slices of bread. Make a batter of milk, eggs, flour and the rest of the sugar. Pour over the contents of the baking dish and dot with butter slices. Place in a pre-heated 375 degree oven for one hour. Serve as is or with cream (heavy or whipped)

# RHUBARB PIE

**2 cups All purpose flour**
**1 teaspoon Salt**
**1 Cup Lard (Must use Lard DO NOT SUBSTITUTE)**
**4-6 tablespoons Ice Cold Water**

Sift together flour and salt. Use a pastry blender to cut lard into flour. Sprinkle ice cold water over dough. Gently gather dough together to form 2 balls. Chill. Roll out 1 ball of dough. Gently gather dough to form 2 balls. Chill. Roll out 1 ball of dough and use for the bottom of the pie. Roll out other ball of dough. Cut rolled dough into twelve ½ inch wide strips. Reserve strips to form a woven lattice for top of pie.

**2 cups Rhubarb, clean and diced**
**2/3 cup Sugar**
**2 tablespoons Flour**
**2 Egg Yolks**
**2 teaspoons Lemon Juice**
**1/8 teaspoon Salt**

Clean and dice rhubarb and set aside. Beat together the sugar, flour, egg yolks, lemon juice, and salt. Place diced rhubarb in bottom of unbaked 9 inch pie pan. Pour sugar-egg mixture over rhubarb in pie pan. Cover top of pie with woven lattice made of pie dough. Allow dough to hang ½ inches over edge of pie pan. Trim off excess dough. Use fingers to crimp dough all around perimeter of pie. Bake at 400 degrees for 20 minutes. Reduce temperature to 350 degrees and bake 20 minutes longer. Remove from oven and cool on wire rack. Cut pie into 6-8 wedges and place each slice on a dessert plate.

# GINGER CRINKLE COOKIES

1 ½ cups lard or shortening
2 cups granulated sugar
2 eggs, large
½ cup Molasses
2 tsps. Ginger
2 tsps. Cloves
2 tsps. Cinnamon
1 tsp. Salt
1 T plus 1 tsp. Baking Soda

Cream together lard (shortening) sugar, eggs, molasses, ginger, cloves, cinnamon, salt, and baking soda.

**4 cups All purpose flour, sifted**
**Additional granulated sugar enough in which to roll balls**

Gradually stir in flour and mix well. Chill dough. Form dough into 48 balls. Roll each ball in granulated sugar. Evenly space sugar coated balls of dough onto lightly greased cookie sheet. Flatten each ball slightly with palm of your hand.

Bake at 350 degrees for about 10-15 minutes OR until light brown. Watch closely so cookies do not burn. Cookies will flatten and crinkle while baking. Yield 4 dozen.

# CHOCOLATE SPICE CAKE

**1 Cup granulated Sugar**
**½ cup Lard or shortening**
**1 tsp Cinnamon, ground**
**1 tsp Allspice**
**2 tablespoons Cocoa Powder**

Place sugar, lard (or shortening), cloves, cinnamon, allspice and ½ teaspoon cloves, ground cocoa powder in large mixing bowl. Cream well until all ingredients are well mixed.

**1 Egg**

Add egg and beat well.

**1 ½ cups all purpose flour, sifted**
**1 teaspoon Baking Soda**
**1 cup Buttermilk**

Sift flour with baking soda. Add flour to creamed mixtures alternately with buttermilk, beginning and ending with the flour. Mix well with each addition. Pour batter into two 8 inch round greased and floured cake pans. Bake 350 degees for 25-30 minutes. Remove from oven, cool. Frost layers, top and sides with Chocolate Fudge Icing (see Below)

**½ cup Butter**
**¾ cup Cocoa Powder**
**4 cups Powdered Sugar, sifted**
**1 teaspoon Salt**
**2/3 cup Milk, scalded**
**Vanilla**

Melt together butter and cocoa powder. Place sifted powdered sugar and salt in large mixing bowl. Scald milk by heating it over medium temperature until milk comes to a rolling boil. Watch carefully so it does not boil over. Pour scalded milk over powdered sugar and stir until dissolved. Beat in vanilla and melted butter-chocolate mixture. Continue beating until thick enough to spread. Frost layers, top and sides.

# APPLE FRITTERS

**Ingredients to serve 4:**
**For the Batter:**
**2 egg yolks**
**1 egg white, beat until stiff**
**½ cup beer**
**3 T sugar**
**2/3 cup all purpose flour**
**1 T butter, melted**
**½ t salt**

Beat together egg yolks, beer, flour and salt. Gradually add flour until batter will stick to a spoon. Add the melted butter and let stand 30 minutes. Stir in the beaten egg white and proceed immediately to process apple slices.

**Remaining Ingredients:**
**4 Large, crisp apples, cored, peeled and sliced (about two inches thick)**
**Cooking oil for deep fat frying**
**Confectioners' sugar**

Just before the 30 minutes are up, begin heating the cooking oil. Dip the apple slices, one at a time in the batter and deep fat fry (a few slices at a time) in the hot oil. Turn slices each once so that they are a golden brown on each side. Remove with a slotted spoon and place on paper towel. Sprinkle with confectioners' sugar. Serve warm.

# CRULLERS

3 egg yolks
2 cups flour
4 T sugar
4 T cream
2 T butter, softened
1 T finely grated lemon or orange peel
optional: 2 T brandy or cognac

Mix together all ingredients, thoroughly, adding the flour last. Work into a dough; refrigerate 3 hours. Roll the dough into a thin sheet, no more than ¼ inch. Cut the sheet of dough into strips about 3 inches long and ½ inch wide. Make a slit in the middle of each piece (about 1 inch long). Pull one end of each strip through the slit. Cook in hot oil until crispy-brown. Sprinkle with sugar (regular or powdered).

# JELLY ROLL

**2 eggs**
**1 cup flour**
**2 T butter, melted**
**½ cup sugar**
**2 T starch**
**¼ cup hot water**
**1 t baking powder**
**jam filling of your choice**

Beat the eggs and sugar until fluffy; add water and beat another minute. Mix together the flour, starch and baking powder. Sift into the liquid and stir in. Place waxed paper on a cookie sheet. Spread the dough evenly on the waxed paper (about ½ inch thick) and bake in a hot oven (about 450 degrees) for about 5 minutes or until brown. Remove from oven. Spread out another piece of waxed paper; sprinkle sugar on it. Turn the cake onto the paper with sugar on it. Remove the top paper (the first paper) and spread the cake with a layer of preserves of your choosing. Roll the cake up and let cool. Scandinavians traditionally served the jelly roll with whipped cream.

# RHUBARB CAKE

2 cups rhubarb, cleaned, scraped and cut into ½ inch chunks
2 eggs
4 T butter, melted
4 T sugar
1 ½ cups flour
3 cups milk
dash of salt

Saute the rhubarb briefly in the melted butter. Spread evenly over the bottom of a greased baking dish. Meanwhile, combine all other ingredients into a batter. Pour the batter over the rhubarb. Bake in a medium oven. Serve with whipped cream topping or sprinkle with sugar while the cake is still hot.

# GLORIFIED RICE

1 cup white rice
1 cup whipping cream, whipped (add sugar to taste)
1 small can crushed pineapple
2 cups water
2 T butter
2 T sugar
salt to taste (start with ½ t)

Bring the water to a boil in a saucepan. Add the rice and butter. Let simmer about 20 minutes, covered. Let cool. Stir in the salt, whipped cream, pineapple and additional sugar to taste. The cream may be added following cooking and served as a hot side dish.

# STUFFED APPLES

**4 large apples (preferably a hard variety)**
**your favorite jam**
**3 eggs, separated**
**3 T sugar**
**2 T ground nuts (of your choice)**

Peel and core the apples. Stuff them with the jam. Beat the egg yolks and sugar together. Beat the whites until stiff and add to the yolks. Pour over apples and then sprinkle each apple with the ground nuts. Bake in a 400 degree oven or about 20 minutes.

# FILBUNKE (FERMENTED MILK)

**1 quart milk**
**6 T fermented milk**
**6 T heavy cream**

Heat the milk to the boiling point, then remove from heat and let cool to room temperature. Stir in fermented milk and cream. Pour into serving bowls; let stand overnight. Refrigerate before serving. Sprinkle nutmeg on surface.

# BREAD PUDDING

**2 cups bread crumbs (either white or rye)**
**1 cup apples, grated or finely chopped**
**juice of 1 orange**
**4 T sugar**
**1 cup whipping cream**

Whip the cream and set it aside. Mix together all ingredients except orange juice. Add this a little at a time, stirring it in (to prevent soaking just a part of the mixture). Serve topped with the whipped cream.

# LINGONBERRY SAUCE

**Use 1 ¼ pounds of sugar to every 2 pounds of berries.**

Add sugar a little at a time, stirring and crushing the berries at the same time. When the sugar has been dissolved and the berries are a juicy pulp, they are ready to be served. Serve chilled.

# ROMME GROT

*Courteously of Avis Sandland*

**1 qt thick sweet cream**
**1 cup flour**
**2 cups warm milk**
**1 t salt**
**Cinnamon and sugar to sprinkle on top**

Bring cream to a boil for about 15 minutes. Gradually sift flour into the cream, mix with a wire whip until very smooth. Allow to simmer, skimming off the fat as it separates. After most of the fat has been skimmed off, add the warm milk and stir until smooth. Add the salt. Pour into bowls and sprinkle top with sugar and cinnamon. Pour the fat over it.

# CHEESECAKE

*Crust:*
**1 cup graham cracker crumbs**
**½ stick butter, melted**
**4 T brown sugar**
**Ingredients for filling:**
**16oz. cream cheese- softened (You may use more than one variety of cheese)**
**4 eggs, beaten**
**1 cup sugar**
**1 T vanilla extract**

*Topping:*
**Whipped cream or an envelope of topping mix**

Combine crust ingredients and press onto the bottom of a lightly greased pie tin or oval baking dish. Bake 15 minutes in a pre-heated 300 degree oven. Let cool.

Combine the filling ingredients in a mixing bowl at low speed. Pour over crust. Bake one hour in a pre-heated 300 degree oven. Let cool. Then run a knife around the edges. Refrigerate at least two hours, then top with whipped cream or prepare topping mix according to directions on the package.

Option: Mince a chocolate bar or sprinkle powder from a chocolate drink-like cocoa over topping.

# PEARS IN HONEY AND PINE NUT CARAMEL WITH ARTISANAL CHEESE

¼ cup (1/2 stick) unsalted butter
3 firm but ripe Bosc pears or other pears, peeled, halved lengthwise, cored
3 ½ tablespoons mild honey (such as orange blossom or clover)
4 ounces artisanal cheese (such as Point Reyes Original Blue, Humboldt Fog, dry Monterey Jack, sheep's-milk ricotta, tangy soft fresh goat cheese, or other local cheese), sliced or crumbled, room temperature
3 tablespoons plus pine nuts
Pinch of fine sea salt

Cook unsalted butter in large nonstick skillet over medium-high heat until beginning to brown. Add pear halves, cut side down, to skillet. Drizzle honey over pears and swirl pan slightly to blend butter and honey. Reduce heat to medium, cover, and cook until pears are tender when pierced with a paring knife, swirling skillet occasionally and adding a few tablespoons water to skillet if caramel sauce turns deep amber before pears are tender, about 12 minutes.

Transfer pears, cut side up, to serving platter. Top pears with cheese. Return skillet with caramel sauce to medium-high heat; add pine nuts to skillet and sprinkle lightly with sea salt. Cook until sauce in skillet is brown and bubbling, about 2 minutes. Spoon sauce over pears and serve.

# CHOCOLATE AMARETTI TORTES

*Tortes:*

**4 ounces semisweet chocolate, chopped**
**¾ cup sliced almonds, toasted**
**12 1½ inch- diameter amaretti cookies**
  **(Italian macaroons), about 2.6 ounces total**
**¼ teaspoon cinnamon**
**Pinch of salt**
**1/2 cup unsalted butter, room temperature**
**½ cup sugar**
**3 large eggs**

*Topping:*

**¾ cup chilled whipping cream**
**1 ½ teaspoons powdered sugar**
**½ teaspoon almond extract**
**2 amaretti cookies, crumbled**

Position rack in center of oven and preheat to 350 degrees F. Butter four 3/4 cup custard cups or soufflé dishes. Dust with flour; tap out excess. Line bottom of cups with parchment paper rounds. Place on rimmed baking sheet.

Stir chocolates in top of double boiler set over simmering water until melted and smooth. Using on/off turns, blend almonds, amaretti, cinnamon, and salt in processor until finely ground. Transfer with spatula, gently stir egg mixture into butter mixture (batter will be thick). Spoon batter into prepared pan; smooth top (cake will be thin). Sprinkle pine nuts over top; press lightly to adhere.

Bake cake until tester inserted into center comes out clean, about 30 minutes. Transfer cake to rack. Run small knife around cake edges to loosen. Remove pan sides. Cool cake completely. (Can be made 1 day ahead. Cover and store at room temperature.)

Sprinkle cake with powdered sugar. Serve with poached fruit.

# CHEESECAKE WITH A TOUCH OF CHOCOLATE

24-28 ounces vanilla wafers
32-36 ounces cream cheese (softened)
8 t cocoa or other chocolate powder
1 cup sugar
1 cup sour cream
4 eggs, beaten
2 cups whipping cream
4 T hot water

In a lightly greased pie tin or baking dish, make a layer of vanilla wafers. In half the hot water, dissolve half the cocoa and spread over the wafers. Make a second layer of wafers and dissolve the rest of the cocoa n the rest of the hot water and spread over this second layer.

Combine the cream cheese, sour cream, sugar and eggs with a mixer- at slow speed. Spread this mixture over the layers of wafers. Bake in a 300 degree oven for one hour. Refrigerate overnight.

Beat whipping cream until stiff and spread over cheesecake before serving.

# CHEESE PUDDING WITH GRAPES

1 pound ricotta or other soft cheese
3 T butter, melted
3 eggs
2 T bread crumbs
6 T sugar
½ t cinnamon
4 T crushed walnuts or pecans (toasted optional)
3 cups grapes-seedless (your choice of color)
2 T wine vinegar
½ t salt

Brush some of the butter on the inside of a 10 inch pie plate. Coat inside of pie plate wth bread crumbs.

Using a blender, combine the cheese, eggs, salt, cinnamon, and half the sugar. Blend until smooth. Pour mixture into pie plate. Sprinkle surface with crushed nuts. Bake in pre-heated 375 degree oven for 25 minutes or until golden.

In the meantime, combine the remainder of the sugar and melted butter and wine vinegar in a baking dish and toss grapes (may be halved- your choice) until well coated. After removing pudding from oven to let cool, bake grapes 10 minutes- shaking a few times.

When grapes have cooled, serve with pudding.

# ORANGES IN CUSTARD SAUCE

10 naval oranges (remove peel and pith and
   cut into thin cross-sections)
1 ½ cups sugar
¾ cup water
¼ t lemon juice

*Custard Sauce:*
4 eggs, yolk only
¼ cup sugar
4 T flour, all-purpose
1 cup milk
1 t vanilla
2 T liqueur (maraschino if available)

Cut oranges and set aside. Make a syrup by boiling the sugar and lemon juice in the water. Boil until the sugar is dissolved and the liquid becomes syrupy.

Beat together the egg yolk and sugar; add flour; stir together. Meanwhile, heat milk to boiling point, but do not let boil. Add hot milk to egg mixture. Cook over low heat, stirring all the while until it thickens. Do not boil. Stir in the liqueur and vanilla.

Chill oranges and custard sauce for at least 8 hours. Pour custard over oranges when served.

# CREAM CAKE

*For cake:*
2 cups heavy cream
6 eggs, separated
1 t baking soda
½ stick butter, softened
2 cups sugar
½ cup extra-virgin olive oil
2 cups flour (all purpose)
1 t vanilla extract

*For frosting:*
1 pound cream cheese, softened
3 cups confectioners sugar
6 T butter, softened
1 ½ t vanilla extract
1 cup chopped walnuts (or nuts of your choice)

Lightly grease 3-10 inch cake pans. Beat egg whites until stiff. Combine with cream and baking soda.

Combine sugar (granulated), butter and oil in a mixer. Add egg yolks one at a time, mixing them in thoroughly. Add cream mixture and flour alternately. Stir in vanilla and egg whites. Pour into 3 pans. Bake 30 minutes in a pre-heated 300 degree oven. A wood toothpick inserted in middle will come out clean if done. Let pans cool on a wire rack 15 minutes, then turn cakes out of pans on rack. Let cool.

Prepare frosting by combining cream cheese and butter (beat until smooth). Still using the mixer, blend in confectioners' sugar and vanilla. Spread frosting between layers and on top and sides of the cake. Scatter with nuts. Refrigerate.

# FLAN DE COCO (COCONUT FLAN)

**1 can condensed milk**
**1 can evaporated milk**
**½ cup sugar**
**½ cup milk**
**½ cup fresh coconut, shredded**
**6 eggs**

Combine all ingredients in an electric blender for 3 minutes. Pour mixture in caramelized Pyrex dish and bake in a double boiler at 350 F for 45 minutes or until knife comes out clean. Let cool, run knife around the edge of the dish to separate it from the sides.

Refrigerate.

# ROSQUILLAS DE MAICENA (CORNSTARCH COOKIES)

**2 cups flour**
**2 tablespoons cornstarch**
**1 egg**
**1 cup butter or margarine**
**1 cup sugar**

Preheat oven 325 F.

Combine all ingredients, mix to form a smooth dough. Roll into long strips ¼ inch thick. Cut with knife into 2 inch lengths, and form a ring with each piece. Place the rings on an ungreased cookie sheet and sprinkle with sugar. Bake at 325 F for 8 to 10 minutes. If desired, sprinkle with cinnamon. About 3 dozen.

# TAMAL DE ELOTE (CORN PUDDING)

1 can condensed milk
3 can whole kernel corn
3 eggs
1 cup melted butter or margarine
1 teaspoon cinnamon

Preheat oven to 350 F.

Combine all ingredients n an electric blender and blend for three minutes. Pour  into a greased Pyrex dish and bake at 350F for 45 minutes or until the knife comes out clean. Serve chilled.

# CAJETA DE COCO (COCONUT FUDGE)

2 cups condensed milk
1 cup fresh coconut meat, shredded
1 cup butter or margarine
½ cup Maria cracker crumbs (graham cracker)
½ teaspoon vanilla

Combine all ingredients in a pan and cook on low heat, stirring constantly with a wooden spoon. Continue cooking 5-6 minutes after a boil has been reached. Form small ball and place on paper cups. 20-30 Fudge Balls.

# ARROZ CON LECHE (RICE CUSTARD)

2 cups rice
1 can condensed sweetened milk
1 can evaporated milk
2 cinnamon sticks
2 whole cloves
Dash of salt
3 cups water

Cook rice in salted water until tender. Add remaining ingredients and mix with a fork, simmer for 15 minutes. Serve warm.

*Variations*
½ cup canned pineapple
½ cup shredded coconut
½ cup raisins
Top with marmalade
Sprinkle with cinnamon

# CAJETA DE LECHE (MILK FUDGE)

**1 can condensed milk**
**1 cup powdered milk**
**1 ½ tablespoons butter or margarine**

Combine all ingredients and stir with a wooden spoon until smooth. Form small balls and place them in small paper cups*. With a knife cut a cross on the top of each ball. In the center of the cross place one of the following:

**Whole clove**
**Piece of macadamia nut**
**Slice of almond**
**Piece of candied fruit**

*Traditionally the balls were placed on lemon leaves to absorb the lemon flavor.

# TRES LECHES (MILK CAKE)

*Cake Base:*
**5 eggs**
**1 teaspoon baking powder**
**1 cup sugar**
**½ teaspoon vanilla**
**1 ½ cups flour**
**butter or margarine**

Preheat oven to 350 F. Sift flour and baking powder. Set aside. Cream butter and sugar until fluffy. Add eggs and vanilla, beat well. Add flour to the butter mixture 2 tablespoons at a time, until well blended. Pour into greased rectangular Pyrex dish and bake at 350 F for 30 minutes. Let cool. Pierce with a fork all over.

*Filling:*
**2 cups milk**
**1 can condensed milk**
**1 can evaporated milk**

Combine the 3 milks and pour over the cool cake.

*Topping:*
**1 ½ cups half & half**
**1 teaspoon vanilla**
**1 cup sugar**

Whip together until thick. Spread over the top of the cake.

Keep refrigerated.

# SHARLOTKA

1 loaf dark bread, without crust and preferably stale
 6-8 tart apples, minced
½ cup butter
½ cup sugar
½ cup red wine or slightly sweetened water
1 teaspoon lemon juice
½ teaspoon vanilla
1 teaspoon grated orange rind
Cinnamon
Dash of salt

Crumble the bread into tiny pieces and fry them slightly in butter. Remove from heat; add wine or sweetened water, lemon juice, sugar and orange rind. Mix well. Add vanilla. Grease a mold and sprinkle lightly with bread crumbs. Place dark bread mixture alternately with minced apples in the mold, sprinkling cinnamon over each layer of apples. The first and the last layer should be bread mixture. Bake in a slow oven (275-300 degrees) for 50-60 minutes. Remove from the mold while still hot and serve at once. You may serve it with any fruit sauce or with plain sweet cream. Or serve it just as it is. Serves four to six people.

# TRADITIONAL EASTER DESSERT (PASKHA)

2 1/2 pounds dry cottage cheese (the cottage cheese must be very dry)
5 large eggs
½ pound melted butter
1 pound sugar
½ pint sour cream
1 teaspoon vanilla
½ pound almonds, blanched and shredded
½ cup candied orange or lemon peel or mixture of both
½ cup seedless raisins

Combine milk, vanilla and salt and bring to a boil. Slowly add farina or semolina or cream of wheat, stirring constantly, and cook over a low flame until the mixture thickens. Beat egg yolks with sugar until very light and beat farina or semolina or cream of wheat into the egg mixture. Add raisins and cook over very low fire for 2-4 more minutes. Grease and sprinkle with sugar a mold and fill it with prepared kasha. Bake in a hot oven (475-500 degrees) for just a few minutes, to melt and caramelize the sugar. Remove kasha from the mold, place on a shallow baking dish or a platter (or on a pie tin) and decorate the top and the sides of kasha with canned fruits, thoroughly drained. Sprinkle generously with sugar all over the place under a broiler for a few minutes. Watch that the kasha doesn't burn. Just before serving, if you like the flavor of kirsch, you may sprinkle it over the kasha and set it aflame. But this has been mainly an American innovation. Serve with apricot or cherry sauce (1/2 cup apricot or cherry preserve mixed with ½ cup warm water and 1 tablespoon rum or any liqueur). Serve hot.

# BLUEBERRY KISEL

**1 ½ pounds blueberries**
**1 ¼ cups sugar**
**2 teaspoons grated lemon rind**
**Potato starch or cornstarch (1 tablespoon of starch for each 2 cups of liquid)**

Prepare the berries by using only the perfect ones. Add just enough water to cover them and cook over a slow fire for 10-15 minutes. Force the berries and the juice through a fine sieve and add sugar and lemon rind. Bring to a quick boil. Measure the mixture and use one tablespoon of starch for two cups of liquid. Dissolve the starch in a small amount of cold water, then add one cup of the berry juice. Mix well and combine with the rest of the berry mixture. Bring to a boil again and remove from the fire. Pour into individual serving dishes and chill for a few hours. Serve with cold milk or cream. This kisel is particularly beneficial to convalescing persons and to children recuperating from upset stomachs. It is very light and yet it is binding.

# CRANBERRY OR LINGONBERRY MOUSSE

1 ¼  cups cranberries or lingonberries
1 ¼ cups sugar
3 ¾  cups water
3 tablespoons cream of wheat or farina or semolina

Place washed and sorted berries in a sack or cheesecloth, folded several times. Put in a pot and squash thoroughly. Add one-cup lukewarm water and squeeze all the liquid out. Place the resulting juice in the refrigerator for further use.

# STUFFED BAKED APPLES

**6 large tart apples**
**¼ cup seedless raisins**
**¼ cup shredded almonds**
**1/3 cup cooked rice (preferably cooked in milk)**
**1/3 cup sugar**
**1 egg**
**2 tablespoons butter**
**Syrup-raspberry or black currant**

Core the apples and carefully remove part of the apples' meat, making sure that the outside of the apples remains without any cuts. Combine raisins, almonds, rice, and add melted butter. Slightly beat egg with sugar and combine with the rest of the ingredients. Fill the centers of the apples with the stuffing and place the apples in a baking dish. Add 6 tablespoons of boiling water and bake in a moderate oven (375°) until tender, basting with the syrup from the bottom of the baking dish. As soon as the apples are ready, place them on a serving platter and cool. Serve with raspberry or blackcurrant syrup or with any of your favorite preserves.

# APRICOT CREAM "CRIMEAN DELIGHT"

¾ cup apricot pulp
½ cup whipping cream
1 cup milk
1/3 cup sugar
3 eggs, separated
½ teaspoon vanilla
1 teaspoon lemon juice
1 envelope unflavored gelatin

Dissolve gelatin in a small amount of lukewarm water. Beat egg yolks with sugar and slowly add milk, stirring constantly. Cook in a double boiler until the mixture thickens, stirring all the time. Add gelatin and stir until it is completely dissolved. Cool. Add apricot pulp. (Prepare the fruit by crushing it and forcing it through a fine sieve. Or you may use canned apricots. Force them through a sieve also.) Add vanilla and lemon juice. Beat the egg whites until very stiff. Beat the whipped cream until very stiff and combine the two. Fold into the egg-yolk mixture and gently stir. Place in a mold (or individual molds) and thoroughly chill for several hours.